BEN-GURION
BUILDER OF ISRAEL

BEN-GURION
BUILDER OF ISRAEL

Robert St. John

London Publishing Company
Washington, D.C.

Published by:

London Publishing Company
1156 15th Street, NW
Suite 510
Washington, DC 20005
(202) 296-7340

Library of Congress Cataloging-in-Publication Data

St. John, Robert, 1902-
     Ben-Gurion : builder of Israel / Robert St. John : foreword
by Avishay Braverman.
          p.   cm.
     Previously published : Washington, D.C. : B'nai B'rith Books,
c1986. With new material.
     Summary: A biography of the first prime minister of Israel,
  with a section that presents Ben-Gurion in his own words.
     ISBN 0-9613262-4-7
     1. Ben-Gurion, David, 1986-1973--Juvenile literature. 2.
Prime ministers--Israel--Biography--Juvenile literature. 3. Zionists--
Palestine--Biography--Juvenile literature. [1. Ben-Gurion, David,
1886-1973. 2. Statesman. 3. Prime ministers. 4. Zionists.]
I. Title
DS125.3.B37S3   1998
956.9405'092--dc21
        [B]
                                                    98-16321
                                                      CIP
                                                       AC

Manufactured in the United States of America

To those Israelis who are striving to keep alive the principles to which Ben-Gurion devoted his life, this book is dedicated.

CONTENTS

FOREWORD

This year, Israel celebrates the fiftieth anniversary of independence. On May 14, 1948, our nation's greatest leader, David Ben-Gurion, declared that the State of Israel had come into being. This engaging book by Robert St. John celebrates Ben-Gurion's life and times.

Robert St. John is my friend, and I never ceased to be amazed at the accomplishments of this world famous author and journalist, who is now in his ninety-seventh year. At Ben-Gurion University of the Negev, we prominently display a bust of Robert St. John in the Aranne Library and Study Center in recognition of his lifetime writing accomplishments, his great admiration for David Ben-Gurion, and his steadfast dedication to Israel's well-being. Together with his wife Ruth, the St. Johns have been among the most devoted friends of our country and this university. They serve as the Honorary Co-Chairs of our Mid-Atlantic South Region of the American Associates of Ben-Gurion University of the Negev.

Robert St. John's definitive biography of David Ben-Gurion was written for young readers. In this edition of *Ben-Gurion: Builder of Israel,* you will also find a section, "In His Own Words," where there are a number of Ben-Gurion quotations on important issues. Reading them today reminds us of the insight and the imposing wisdom of Israel's legendary leader.

In a second special part of this book, I invite you to read about Ben-Gurion University, and our efforts to make the university a worthy legacy of David Ben-Gurion's vision to build a "Hebrew Oxford in the Negev."

Finally, I would like to acknowledge the commitment of loyal supporters of our university, Margery and Sheldon London, to insure that this expanded new edition of Robert St. John's book would be available to celebrate Israel's fiftieth anniversary.

PROFESSOR AVISHAY BRAVERMAN
PRESIDENT, BEN-GURION UNIVERSITY OF THE NEGEV
BEER-SHEVA, ISRAEL

CHAPTER ONE

David Ben-Gurion was the man who did more than anyone else to make an old, old dream of the Jews come true—the dream of Israel—the dream of having a Jewish state again, in the same place their ancestors used to live.

As a reward for what he did, and because he was such a strong leader, he was made Israel's first Prime Minister. Soon he was famous all over the world. People recognized him wherever he went because of the ring of soft white hair around his head and his friendly brown eyes. His jaw was firm and his skin had a ruddy glow. His lips were thin, and he often pressed them together when he was thinking about something important. But when he was happy his eyes twinkled and his smile was cheerful and sunny.

He always moved his hands when he was talking. He thumped his desk and tapped the arm of his chair, and sometimes he pointed to the person he was talking to if he wanted that person to listen carefully to what he was saying.

He liked to wear loose trousers, comfortable shoes, and a shirt open at the neck. Sometimes, because he was the Prime Minister, he had to wear a tall silk hat and striped trousers and a coat with tails. But he took them off as soon as he could and put his old clothes on again.

The salary he got for being Prime Minister was about four hundred dollars a month. That was less money than most New York taxi drivers made.

He did not own an automobile. The government supplied him with an old Dodge, but he decided it was too fancy. He wanted to exchange it for a jeep. However, his doctor did not think this was a good idea.

"A jeep will be very bad for your lumbago," he explained.

"But how can I set an example to other government officials with people like you telling me what to do?" Ben-Gurion demanded.

Finally he agreed to use a small car after he was told it would be cheaper to buy and run than a jeep. But he still would have liked a jeep because it was plainer-looking.

Ben-Gurion was a very plain man. When he became Commander-in-Chief and then Prime Minister he could have covered his chest with medals or put his picture on stamps or ridden in big cars with armed bodyguards. But he did none of these things, because he thought his people should live simply and that as their leader he should set an example for them.

He could laugh at jokes about himself, and there were many. He smiled at the story people were telling just after the 1948 war with the Arabs ended. A man was so tired of standing in line to buy food that he bought a gun and told a friend he was going to shoot Ben-Gurion because he was to blame for all of Israel's troubles. A few days later the friend met the unhappy man again and asked him what had happened.

"Well," he said, "I bought the gun and went to Ben-Gurion's office, but there were so many people already standing in line waiting to shoot him that I got discouraged and went home."

Ben-Gurion was famous for his ability to read quickly. When Israel was a new country and he had thousands of problems, a friend lent him a book of philosophy. It was four hundred pages long. Two days later he returned it.

"Maybe you would like to borrow it later, when you have more time," the friend said.

The Prime Minister smiled. He had read the whole book, and proved it by telling his friend all about it.

He always tried to keep his promises, even when he made them to people who were not famous or important. During the war he promised Josef, one of his messengers, that he would go to his wedding. But at the last minute his army officers needed him and he couldn't go. So when Josef came home from his honeymoon, Ben-Gurion said to him:

"I've missed your wedding, but at least I will not be kept from having wine and cakes with you. I will come to your house tomorrow at ten."

At a quarter to ten the next morning the Prime Minister looked at his watch, then turned to the members of his Cabinet and said:

"I am sorry but I must go now to see Josef and his wife. I will be back in an hour."

He was a brave man. When he knew he was right about something, nothing could make him change his mind, not even riots by gangs or threats to kill him.

He would never forgive lying, but he would give a second chance to a man who has made a mistake.

He understood the hopes and dreams of the *sabras*—the young people who have been born in Israel. He chose only young people for his personal staff and loved to give them problems to test them out.

He read the Bible often, for it reminded him of the long history of his people. It reminded him how important they were, and still are.

Sometimes he was amazingly patient. He could sit in a government meeting for hours, silent, while the others lost their tempers and argued. When they had finally tired themselves, Ben-Gurion would get up and quietly tell them what it was best to do.

He didn't waste a minute. He was always on time for his appointments and complained if someone else was tardy. "The only thing you can never recover is time," he often said.

He had faults and he made mistakes. Once a member of Israel's Parliament—the Knesset—who had criticized him ended his speech by saying:

"But, after all, only a great man can make great mistakes."

Most of the people who criticized him admitted that there might not be an Israel today if it had not been for David Ben-Gurion.

CHAPTER TWO

In the days when the Czars ruled Russia, Plonsk was a small factory city near Warsaw, Poland, on a river that was also named Plonsk.

In Plonsk one stormy day late in 1886, Sheindal Green, a gentle young woman, presented her husband, Avigdor, with their sixth child.

The sixth child of Sheindal and Avigdor Green became David Ben-Gurion, the first Prime Minister of Israel.

As a boy, David was small for his age, but his head was so large for his body that one day his mother took him to a doctor and nervously asked if there was something wrong with him.

"Calm your fears," the doctor said to Mrs. Green after he had examined David. "Your child is quite all right. But I can tell you this; someday he will be a great man. That is very clear from the shape and size of the skull."

David's father was a lawyer. He was known as

one of the wise men of Plonsk, and many of the Jews of the town came to him for advice. But at the same time he was a rebel. He put aside the long tunic and the fur hat that most of the Jews in Plonsk wore. Instead he wore a frock coat and striped trousers, and sometimes even a high silk hat.

He insisted that David and the rest of his children learn to speak Hebrew as well as they spoke Russian. This displeased the holy men of Plonsk, for they believed Hebrew was for worship alone. You spoke Hebrew when you spoke to God, but you spoke Yiddish when you ordered groceries.

David also had to study Biblical history and Middle Eastern geography. He went to a religious school and was a good pupil; he took himself and his studies very seriously. Once he startled his classmates by announcing:

"One day I will be the leader of Israel."

Mr. Green did not have such a splendid dream for his son, but he did believe that someday his people, the Jews, would return to their ancient homeland. The Greens lived just off the main street in Plonsk, and at all hours of the day and night their house was filled with visitors who came to talk about going back to the Land of Israel. They called themselves Zionists and they called their idea Zionism, since it was their wish to return to Zion, as the land of their ancestors had been named in Biblical times by King David. Now it was called Palestine, a name the Romans had given it when they came as conquerors several thousand years ago. It was a desert country just north of Egypt. Here Jews had lived since their flight from Egypt; only now most of the inhabitants were Arabs, for the Jews had been scattered across the face of the earth, but they were talking more than ever about leaving Russia and returning to Israel because of recent pogroms, the persecution and killing of Jews.

Sometimes David would listen from the next room to the talk about Palestine. Sometimes, instead, he would try to read his books or play a game of chess by himself. It was a game he liked because it taught him how to fix his mind on one problem and shut out everything else.

When David was ten years old, something happened that was important to the Greens and to Jews all over the world. Theodor Herzl, a Jewish reporter for a Viennese paper, wrote a booklet called *The Jewish State.* In it he said the end of persecution of the Jews in Europe because of their religion would come only when a great many of them would move to a place where they could set up a country of their own.

After the Herzl booklet was printed, there were meetings in the Green house more and more often. The talk was louder and lasted longer than ever before. Now there were articles for the newspapers to be written, more committees to be formed, and more meetings.

Two years later, when David was twelve, his mother died. Up to this time he had been a quiet boy and had only a few friends. He had been very close to his gentle mother. Now he had to turn to his father, but his father was a busy man: he had many small children to worry about, his duties as a Zionist, and his work as a lawyer. So more and more David stayed alone with his books, and the people who knew him saw less and less of the gentleness that he had learned from his mother.

That same year, Herzl called a worldwide meeting of Jews in Switzerland to discuss how to make the Zionist dream come true. The gathering caused much excitement, even among the young people of Plonsk. For the first time in almost two thousand years Jews spoke about the return as if they really meant to go back someday soon instead of just talking about it. They discussed building a Hebrew university in Jerusalem and creating a Jewish world bank. They adopted a design for a national flag of blue and white, the colors of the tallit or prayer shawl. A song written in Hebrew called *Hatikvah* or "Our Hope" was to be the national anthem. But, most important of all, these people declared for everyone to hear that their aim was to build a Jewish nation in Palestine based upon the vision of the Ancient Prophets of justice and peace. Any Jew in the world could take part in this great adventure just by saying that he agreed with this aim and by paying one shekel, one mark, one shilling, or one American quarter.

When he was fourteen David and some other teenagers of Plonsk founded a Zionist youth society, named after Ezra, the ancient Biblical priest. The members took an oath that they would never speak any language but Hebrew to each other and that they would try to teach other young people about the ways of the ancient Hebrew people.

The leaders of this society were David and his two closest friends, Shlomo Zemach, whose parents were wealthy, and Shmuel Fuchs, who was eager for adventure. Shmuel was the first to leave Plonsk, but instead of going to Palestine he chose America. Then one autumn night Shlomo left for Palestine—without his father's consent, but with three hundred rubles of his money. David missed his friends, but he was busy now, traveling around Poland, making speeches, and telling more and more people about the plan for a Jewish homeland.

Finally Shlomo came to Plonsk on a visit. He said he would soon be going back to Palestine. Life was hard there, but it was good. Men, women, and children were pouring into Palestine from Europe. However, everything was not yet perfect. It was not easy to get a job. Most of the work in Palestine was being done by Arabs, even if the employers were Jewish.

But he had found a job and was growing used to a diet of bread and dates.

The boys of the youth society listened eagerly while he told them of the ancient land, of the hills surrounding Jerusalem, of camels and mosques and Bedouin thieves who stole in at night from the desert.

One day when he was eighteen David announced to his father that when Shlomo left he was going with him, perhaps never to return. Mr. Green did not like the idea at all. He said it was a disgrace that a boy should stop his studies before he had even an average education. He himself was full of the wisdom of books and he had always hoped that someday his son would be, too. But going off to become a common laborer on the desert sands of Palestine, what sense did that make?

But his father could not persuade him to stay, for Shlomo's tales had made him sure that life in Palestine would be exciting. So together the two boys left Plonsk.

CHAPTER THREE

David and Shlomo stood at the rail of the ship that had brought them from Odessa, a Russian port on the Black Sea, through the Dardanelles, and down the eastern coast of the Mediterranean Sea. Their clothes were stained and they were very weary, but they were staring hard at the horizon because each wanted to be the first to see it. The trip had taken weeks, and now Plonsk was far behind, part of another life.

Suddenly Shlomo cried, "Look, David! There it is. Look hard! Just a little to the left of the bow. That's it. That's Jaffa!"

David stared and finally saw it. It was just a small brown spot, but this was the Promised Land. *His* land. *Eretz Yisrael*, the Land of Israel. Here he would live and die. Here he would make the dream come true for others. He looked over his shoulder at the stern of the ship. There was only the vast green sea.

But someday that sea would be black with a parade of ships bringing his people home again.

Now they could see buildings and figures. Jaffa was a famous old seaport about halfway down the coast of Palestine. The Bible told how it had belonged to the tribe of Dan. Of course, almost every place in this part of the world was famous in Jewish history and mentioned in the Bible. He was glad his father had insisted he learn Middle Eastern history and geography. He knew that within sight of Jaffa, Jonah's ship had been wrecked by the anger of God and Jonah had been cast into the sea, to be swallowed by the whale.

But when they went ashore, David became confused. This was a strange world, not at all as he had pictured it. The streets were full of Arabs in flowing white robes. There were strong smells everywhere. People spoke in a language that sounded a little like Hebrew, yet David didn't understand a word of it. Occasionally two men speaking Yiddish would pass.

David and Shlomo went to a shabby building called the Hotel Chaim Baruch. Here some Zionists were waiting to greet them.

"*L'chaim*! To life!" they shouted together as they raised their glasses of sweet wine. Then David had his first meal in the land of his ancestors.

That night they went to a settlement called Petach Tikvah, one of the first settlements of the *Yishuv*, the Hebrew word for the Zionist settlements of Palestine. It was a pleasant place. There were houses in neat rows, some built of wood, some of mud. Eucalyptus trees lined the roads, and there were large groves of fruit trees. Most important of all, here were Jews who had become farmers.

The boys were tired when they arrived. But David did not fall asleep easily that night. His mind was too full of plans as he lay on his bed, listening to the soft noises of the desert, which was not very far away.

"Who could sleep through his first night in the homeland?" he wrote his father in his first letter. "I smelled the rich odor of corn. I heard the braying of donkeys and the rustle of leaves in the orchards. Above were clusters of stars, clear and bright.... My heart overflowed with happiness...."

The next morning David and Shlomo tried to find jobs. They went from one Jewish farm to another, offering to do any kind of work. But everywhere the answer was the same. The farmers hired Arabs. Arabs worked for less money and they were experienced. But finally David and Shlomo found work on a farm at eight piasters a day, which was only a few cents. This was just enough for them to rent a bed and buy dinner when they finished their day's work.

For a year David worked and sweated in Judea. He was not used to the work, and sometimes he was hungry. He became thin, and for a while he was sick. But still he was indignant at Jews who were too timid or too satisfied where they were to move to Palestine.

When David had been in Palestine about a year he met a young man named Itzhak Ben-Zvi, who had just come from Russia. They liked each other right away, and in the years that followed they became close friends.

By now David could speak Arabic. By now he also knew every part of Judea—every village, every road, and every dried-up stream. But he and Shlomo decided that farming in Judea was not interesting enough. David wanted to be in a place where there were wide fields and the sweet smell of grass. So he made up his mind to go north to Galilee, where there were many Jewish farmers. He and ten other young men walked the whole way, almost sixty miles, and at the little settlement of Sejera he found the place of his dreams. The houses were in rows on a hillside and surrounded by mountains. There were eucalyptus trees and pepper trees, too. The men plowed the fields and planted the seed. The women weeded the gardens and milked the cows, and the children herded the geese and rode on horseback to meet their fathers in the fields.

David loved it here. But there was also trouble in Galilee. The Arabs thought they could force the Jews to leave the land if they bothered them enough—if they burned their buildings, stole their cattle, and attacked travelers on the roads. So the Jews had to protect their property, and themselves. To do this they paid Arab soldiers to stand guard at night. Though this seems strange they did it because they thought that if the Arabs were busy being watchmen they would not steal, and because Jews had not been soldiers for many hundreds of years and did not have much practice in defending themselves.

Almost as soon as David arrived in Sejera he tried to change this. Jewish land everywhere must be guarded by Jewish watchmen, he said. But the men of Sejera shook their heads. If the Jews defended themselves, the Arabs would resent it. If the Arab watchmen lost their jobs they might become angry and set fires in the settlement and rob the people.

David and his friends spied for a few nights and found that the Arab watchmen did no watching at all. Instead they were enjoying themselves in a nearby Arab village. If anything was stolen, they would find it and return it to its owner—if he paid them a large enough reward. Then they would share the reward with the thief.

To prove this to the settlement manager, David and his friends stole the manager's favorite mule one night and hid it. Then they told him it had been stolen. He ran to the stables, found the mule gone, and shouted for the watchman. He was nowhere near. They finally found him asleep in the Arab village. So he was fired and one of David's friends was given the job.

This was the beginning of Jewish self-defense in

Palestine. The Arabs made raids on Sejera to frighten the people. David said the Jews must be organized to defend themselves and that they must get weapons. But they did not know where to get them.

Then one day the bailiff of the settlement sent a wagon to the city of Haifa. In some mysterious way the wagon came back loaded with old shotguns.

Many years later David still remembered those guns. He said: "We played with them like children; we never let them down for a moment. Reluctantly we went to work next morning, for we had to say good-by to them for a whole day. As soon as we got home and unharnessed our horses and mules we dashed off to our beloved rifles, and they never left our hands until we fell asleep. Rifle in hand or on shoulder, we ate and washed, we moved and read or talked."

So they worked by day and stood guard by night, and they plowed the land with rifles slung across their backs. They were traveling the hard road of Zionism. There would be no turning back now. They knew that. Jewish blood would have to be spilled in defense of these fields before the fight for their homeland would be won.

Not everyone agreed with David about this. Shlomo, for one, was against the idea of Jewish self-defense. He and David shared a room, and they argued long into every night. Shlomo said that all of them had returned to the land of the Bible to lead a peaceful life in the place where they belonged. If they stirred up the Arabs, there would be no *shalom*, no peace, ever.

David answered that they were in the Middle East now, not Europe. The law of the desert was the only law the Arabs understood. The law of the desert meant defending yourself. Palestine belonged to Turkey, but the authority of the Turkish Government had almost disappeared. Murderers were seldom punished, and thieves were free to steal.

David convinced most of the settlers that he was right, but not Shlomo, for Shlomo went to Paris to study and did not return for many years.

About this time Ben-Zvi , who was living in Jerusalem, sent David a message saying: "Come at once!"

David did not like cities very much. He had seen a few of them: Warsaw, Odessa, Constantinople. But perhaps Jerusalem was different. Jerusalem was the city of David. David the King had made it one of the illustrious cities of the world. There Solomon had built the Temple with cedars from Lebanon and had adorned it with gold. Today Jerusalem belonged to the empire of the Turks. Still, there were Jews there. Ben-Zvi was there. He wrote that he was going to start a weekly Zionist newspaper in Hebrew, to be called *Ha'achdut*, which means *The Unity*, and he desperately needed David's help.

David insisted that he was a farmer now, that he belonged on the land, but Ben-Zvi said it was his duty to come. Finally David said he would, and not long afterward he settled down in Jerusalem. Now he was one of the editors of *Ha'achdut*. His first article for the paper was signed "Ben-Gurion." This was the first time he used the name by which the whole world someday would know him. He chose it because it sounded like a name out of the Bible. "Ben" is Hebrew for "son of." "Gurion" means "young lion." So he was David, son of the young lion. From now on he would be David Ben-Gurion, citizen of Israel, a country that existed only in the dreams of a few idealistic Jews.

He was almost twenty-four years old, a handsome young man with black wavy hair. His dark mustache was trimmed in the latest Turkish style, with upturned points. He wore a suit with a high-buttoned waistcoat, a white shirt, and a striped silk tie with a very large knot. He looked as if he might have been a newspaperman from London or New York.

He had found it easy to like the soil and become a farmer. Now he found it was even easier to like being a journalist. So, although he would become famous as a statesman and a soldier, for the rest of his life he would always refer to himself as a "journalist."

Once, after he had become Prime Minister, a reporter from a foreign country asked him for some information for an article he was going to write. "I'm using that information in an article of my own," he growled. "Don't forget, I'm a journalist, too!"

CHAPTER FOUR

Ben-Gurion stayed in Jerusalem for three years, and at the end of that time he was more certain than ever that he must prepare himself to lead the Jews of Palestine. So he made up his mind to go to Constantinople, the capital of the Turkish Empire, to learn Turkish and study law.

He and Ben-Zvi talked about it. Ben-Zvi wanted to go, too. They agreed that Ben-Gurion would go first and Ben-Zvi would follow soon afterward. *Ha'achdut* now had a large staff. Others could carry on while they were away.

Ben-Gurion left and was soon joined in Constantinople by Ben-Zvi. Their friends began to call them "the Twins," for they both wore red fezes, black frock coats, and black ties. One by one, other young men came, among them Joseph Trumpeldor, so tall that he made Ben-Gurion look like a small boy. These two liked each other instantly. During the Russo-Japanese War Trumpeldor had been the only

Jewish officer in the Czar's Army, because to be an officer a man had to be of noble birth and no Jews were noblemen. He had lost an arm during the fighting. Now he was a settler in Palestine. Even with one arm he could do more work than any of the other settlers. He had taught himself to dress, shave, eat, shoot a gun, and ride a horse, all with one arm.

When they first met, Ben-Gurion looked at the empty sleeve with envy. Here was a Jew brave enough to give an arm, a Jewish war hero!

Together Ben-Gurion and Trumpeldor tramped the streets of Constantinople. It was 1914, and they talked mostly of the war that everyone said was coming, for Germany, Austria, and Turkey were uniting against England, France, and Russia. If war came, would the Turkish Empire be destroyed? If so, then perhaps the Jews of Palestine would have a chance to set up a state of their own.

They all tried to apply themselves to the study of law, but there was the smell of gunpowder in the air. So they went home to Jerusalem on a visit to see how things had been going while they were away.

Panic was spreading among the people in the Holy City. Money was no longer coming from Europe and America. Food shipments were no longer arriving. The Turkish Government had ordered that all healthy men must either be drafted into the Army, go to jail, or leave the country.

Trumpeldor disappeared, and it was said he had gone to fight again for Russia.

In England the most important man among the Zionists was Chaim Weizmann, a famous scientist who had left Russia and moved to London. He was saying that the Zionists should help Great Britain win the war. Ben-Gurion disagreed with him. Great Britain and Russia were allies. If Great Britain won the war, so would Russia. But Ben-Gurion and most of the others who remembered the terrible pogroms that had taken place in Russia secretly hoped that the Russians would lose. In *Ha'achdut* he wrote that Jews not drafted into the Turkish Army should enlist in a special Jewish battalion to defend Palestine.

Trumpeldor popped up in Alexandria, Egypt. So did Vladimir Jabotinsky, a Russian journalist who was also a Zionist. Jabotinsky's feelings against Russia were as strong as Ben-Gurion's, but his hatred of the Turkish Empire was greater. He believed that the empire had to be broken up before the Jewish homeland could be restored.

Jabotinsky and Trumpeldor discussed the idea of a Jewish battalion in the British Army. They thought this might help their people after the war, when the fate of Palestine would be decided. But the British authorities in Egypt would only allow them to form a battalion of mule drivers, "the Zion Mule Corps."

"Never!" Jabotinsky shouted. He was insulted by the very name "Mule Corps."

But Trumpeldor was persuaded by a British general who made him a promise, although he had no authority to do it. The general said there would be a "Jewish Palestine after the war" if Trumpeldor and his men would drive mules loaded with ammunition into the front lines of the Army. So Trumpeldor went off to war with six hundred Jewish mule drivers who bravely helped him do this dangerous job.

Meanwhile in Palestine there was complete disorder. Already thousands of Jews had fled to Egypt, and more were going every day. Turkish police were arresting Jews by the hundreds and sending them to special camps and to prisons.

One day they raided *Ha'achdut's* office, and both Ben-Gurion and Ben-Zvi were thrown into a Jerusalem jail.

A few days later they heard they were to be expelled from the country because they had been plotting to form a Jewish state. From their cell they sent an appeal to Jamal Pasha, the Turkish governor of Palestine.

The jail was more like a shabby hotel than a prison. Ben-Gurion was allowed to attend meetings and keep business appointments outside the jail.

One day he met Jamal Pasha on a Jerusalem street. "I have refused your appeal," the governor said sternly. "You are to be expelled."

So Ben-Gurion and Ben-Zvi went to Egypt. But when they arrived there, they were arrested again, this time by the British. The British said they were enemies, loyal to Turkey, the country that had just expelled them. But many friends came to their aid, and finally they were allowed to go to the United States.

They arrived in New York early in the summer of 1915 and rented rooms in a house near Broadway. One of the first things Ben-Gurion bought was a big English dictionary, which he kept on a stand in the center of his room.

In the first few months he came to like the United States very much. He had never seen Jews anywhere else so free. But he thought many American Jews were too satisfied with themselves, and almost none of them knew Hebrew.

After they had been in the United States a short while, Ben-Gurion and Ben-Zvi went around the country, trying to persuade people to come and live in Palestine. They wanted healthy, idealistic young Zionists who were eager to learn to be good farmers and who would also study Hebrew. They went from state to state. Curious crowds flocked to their meetings, and thousands of Jews said they would come.

Later that year Ben-Gurion met Paula Munweis at a party in New York. She was twenty-three years old, and she had been born in Russia, where her father had been prosperous. She had been thirteen when she arrived in New York. She had wanted to be a doctor, but her father died, and after that she received no more money from Russia, so she became a student nurse instead.

Paula says she was "a plain, very serious-looking girl." Her hair was waved back off her forehead; she wore glasses without rims and dressed in plain dark clothes.

In those days Ben-Gurion dressed in the style of the times. On important occasions he wore a very high stiff collar. His hair was still black and wavy, but he had shaved off his Turkish mustache.

Although Paula was Jewish, she didn't have any interest in Palestine. She was not a "bookish" person, and she was happiest when there were people around. She spoke her mind plainly, never holding anything back.

By contrast, Ben-Gurion liked to be alone. All his thoughts centered in Palestine. Zionism was more important to him than food and comfort. Books were all he ever wanted money for. He always thought carefully before he spoke and often decided that it was wiser to be silent.

Yet they fell in love. Paula was fascinated by the stories of his adventures. But it was his earnestness that won her. He told her that someday there would be a Jewish nation and that he would be one of its leaders.

"I knew from the day I met him that he was a great man," she said. "I could tell that he was like one of the prophets out of the Bible...."

Their wedding was secret. The only person they told about it was Ben-Zvi. Even Paula's sister in Brooklyn didn't know until later. They were married in City Hall, but there was no time for a honeymoon. After the wedding Ben-Gurion rushed off to a meeting and Paula went back to the hospital.

Shortly afterward in London, Jabotinsky finally received permission to form a Jewish Legion. So Ben-Gurion and Ben-Zvi started to enlist American Jews in a Jewish Legion to serve with the British Army. They hoped that many of the soldiers from Canada and the United States would decide to stay in Palestine after they had fought for it.

In November 1916 there came an announcement from Great Britain that caused Zionists all over the world to celebrate wildly. It was the Balfour Declaration. In this famous statement the British Government said that if the Allies won the war, Great Britain, as one of the victorious allies, would view "with favor the establishment in Palestine of a national home for the Jewish people."

The next month Jerusalem was captured from the Turks. It began to look as if better days had arrived for the Jewish people.

In April 1918, Ben-Gurion himself enlisted in the Jewish Legion and several weeks later left with the other volunteers for training in Canada. He had left Paula with her older sister in Brooklyn and promised to write often. That summer he landed in Egypt with his battalion, the 39th Fusiliers.

Ben-Gurion was made a full corporal and Ben-Zvi a lance corporal. They sewed the stripes on their uniforms with as much pride as if they had been decorations from the King. But soon afterward Ben-Gurion became sick and was sent to the hospital. He was there when the wonderful news came from Paula in Brooklyn. He was a father. His daughter Geula had been born.

When Ben-Gurion and Ben-Zvi first saw Palestine again they were shocked at what had happened to the Promised Land. The Turks had been driven out by the British Army, but the Jewish people had suffered greatly during the war. There had been very little food, many people were hungry, and there were not nearly enough hospital beds for those who were sick.

Then Dr. Chaim Weizmann arrived in Jerusalem. Corporal Ben-Gurion decided there were many things he should discuss with the famous Dr. Weizmann. But he was near Tel Aviv and Dr. Weizmann was forty-five miles away in Jerusalem, and Corporal Ben-Gurion's superior officer would not give him permission to leave camp.

But one day he left anyway. He had no trouble getting to Jerusalem, and his visit with Dr. Weizmann was very pleasant. As he was leaving, he told Dr. Weizmann that he was absent without permission.

"I shall arrange with army headquarters here in Jerusalem for an official twenty-four-hour leave for you," Dr. Weizmann assured him.

At the end of the twenty-four hours Corporal Ben-Gurion was back in Tel Aviv. As he entered his tent, two British soldiers arrested him.

"But I was granted a twenty-four-hour leave by Jerusalem headquarters," he argued.

"Yes, we know all about that," one of the soldiers snapped back. "But we're charging you with being absent without leave from the time you left here until you reached Jerusalem."

His corporal's stripes were taken away and he had to spend thirty days confined to the barracks. Then he was sent to another company.

Ben-Gurion's days in the Jewish Legion were not the happiest of his life.

CHAPTER FIVE

In the years that Ben-Gurion had been away from Palestine a few new Jewish leaders had arisen. One was Eliahu Golomb. He was one of the Jews who had offered to fight with the British Army when they came into Palestine. After the war ended, he and Jabotinsky tried to keep the Jewish Legion active, because they were sure that the Jews of Palestine would someday have to fight in order to have a country of their own and would need trained soldiers. But the British, who now were in military control of Palestine, had a different idea, and in a short time there were only a few hundred men left out of the five thousand who had been in the Legion.

So Golomb told everyone who would listen that it was necessary for the Jews to have their own secret army. Ben-Gurion was one of those who listened. He liked this young man with the sharp features and the bright eyes, and soon they became friends.

When Golomb began to form the underground

army called *Haganah*—which means defense—Ben-Gurion and Ben-Zvi helped him because they all believed that the Jews would have to fight for their Promised Land.

About this time Paula and little Geula arrived in Palestine from New York. Paula was not shy, and she was not afraid of work. But Palestine was a frightening place for a young women from New York especially a young women with a small baby. There was dirt everywhere. There seemed to be thousands of flies, and beggars were on every street. People ate strange food, and there was no running water in the houses. Besides all this, most of the people in Palestine spoke Arabic or Hebrew, and Paula knew only English and Yiddish and a little Russian that she remembered from her childhood. Ben-Gurion found them a small apartment in Tel Aviv. This was a new city on the edge of the Mediterranean, built by Jews just a few years before. It was the most modern-looking place anywhere in Palestine, but still it was foreign for Paula. She tried very hard to get used to living in this strange country, but in the beginning she was discouraged.

In the spring of 1920 Great Britain, France, the United States, and the other allied nations that had won World War I had a meeting in the Italian city of San Remo to settle the new order of the Middle East caused by their defeat of the Turkish Empire. One critical question was the future of Palestine.

"What will happen?" Paula asked her husband.

Ben-Gurion shrugged his shoulders. Who knew what would happen?

The Jews of Palestine were nervous while they waited. Then one day an announcement came. Great Britain had been given a 'Class A' mandate over Palestine.

First Paula wanted to know what a mandate was. Ben-Gurion explained to her that some of the Allies were going to be given control over certain countries that had been set free. These countries would be treated like children until they grew up enough to run themselves.

"Class A? What does that mean?" Paula asked.

Ben-Gurion told her. It meant that Great Britain would rule Palestine for only a little while, and then the inhabitants would govern themselves.

The Jews of Palestine went through the streets singing. They drank toasts in red wine. There was dancing, and a little crying, too.

"Israel lives again!" they shouted. "After almost two thousand years!"

But David Ben-Gurion did no celebrating that day. He studied the words of the mandate and wrinkled his brow. Which inhabitants, Arab or Jew would rule in Palestine?

In July the first High Commissioner was sent from England to govern Palestine. He was Sir Herbert Samuel.

Again there was shouting in the streets.

"Do you hear this?" one man would say to another. "A Jew! After two thousand years of waiting, at last a Jew will sit in Jerusalem again and run the country."

Ben-Gurion said nothing, for he wondered: What sort of a Jew is he? Will he help the Jews build their new home? Can we trust him? Let's not celebrate yet.

Soon large numbers of Jewish immigrants were coming into the country, although Palestine was barely ready to receive them.

Again there was rejoicing.

"They will help build our new nation," people said.

But Ben-Gurion saw them crowding into Tel Aviv until the new little city was ready to burst. Only a few were going on to the land to become farmers. Many came with a little money and wanted to start small businesses.

He was disappointed, because he knew that there were already too many businessmen in Palestine. What the country needed was farmers, to turn the brown desert sand into a rich, green countryside. As a teenaged boy he had learned how exciting life on the land could be. He wanted the new immigrants whom he called *Halutzim* or "pioneers" to have this experience, too, and to help build up the agriculture of the country and establish settlements on the uninhabited desert.

When the next Zionist conference was called to meet in London, Ben-Gurion was chosen to be one of the speakers. This was the first international meeting he had ever attended. It was held in The Royal Albert Hall, a place that could seat several thousand people. On the platform were important people: people from New York, Paris, Warsaw—from all over the world. And he, David Ben-Gurion, was on the program.

At this meeting Chaim Weizmann and Ben-Gurion clashed head on for the first time. Weizmann had felt for a long time that there was no hope for a Jewish state except with the help of the British. But Ben-Gurion had grown impatient with the British.

Now in The Albert Hall he listened to speaker after speaker say the Jews should be careful; they should let only a certain number of their people come into Palestine each year. The more he listened, the angrier he grew. Dr. Weizmann seemed to be behind this controversy.

When it was Ben-Gurion's turn to speak, he demanded bold action. He accused Dr. Weizmann's group of standing between the people of Palestine and the new rulers of the country, the British, and preventing the people from telling their rulers what they really wanted. Even when the Turks governed Palestine, he said, they had always been able to go directly to Jamal Pasha, the governor.

Weizmann did not like to be contradicted. He thought Ben-Gurion was headstrong, a troublemaker. Ben-Gurion thought Weizmann was timid, and not sufficiently sensitive to bringing to Palestine all those Jews who wished to come.

Later Paula came to London with Geula, and Ben-Gurion rented a small apartment for them. There Amos, their son, was born.

When Ben-Gurion chose Amos as the baby's name, Paula asked:

"Why Amos?"

So Ben-Gurion told her the story of the Prophet Amos in the Bible. Amos had been a shepherd, and he believed that God was not just for Israel but for all people everywhere. He said God would punish those who were cruel to the poor people in the world. Then he told her Amos had prophesied that the children of Israel someday would return to their own land and that they would have peace and be prosperous.

When the meeting in London was over, Ben-Gurion decided to take Paula and the children with him on a tour of Europe. They went across the English Channel in a ship. This was a trip Paula never forgot. Most of the passengers on the ship were seasick, and she thought longingly of Brooklyn and the comfortable life she had left behind there.

But Paris was exciting. So was Vienna, a city she remembered her mother and father telling her about.

The trip lasted for many weeks, and it was not always pleasant. The trains were dirty, and Paula was alone for many days and many nights in a small hotel room with the children while Ben-Gurion was away making speeches.

Once in a while she would get someone to stay with the children while she went and listened to her husband. He seemed to convince people with his sincerity and his ideals.

They ended their tour in Plonsk. Ben-Gurion's father had married again, and several of the children were still living at home.

"It was the nicest house in Plonsk," Paula said later, for she was impressed with the place where her husband had been born.

CHAPTER SIX

After the British took charge of Palestine, the Jews set up a body called the Jewish Agency, with headquarters in Jerusalem. The British mandate had said that the Agency should represent the Jewish people as they worked toward their independence. The Agency had its own Cabinet, called the Jewish Agency Executive. Ben-Gurion became a member.

The mandate did not say the Jewish Agency could have an Army, but it had one anyway; it had Haganah, the underground army Eliahu Golomb was building. Ben-Gurion had been for it from the beginning.

"We must make the Jews who come back home proud they are Jews," he said. To be proud they had to stop being afraid, and they would stop being afraid when they had a way of striking back at their enemies. The Army would give them this.

In these years Ben-Gurion's wavy dark hair began to grow thin and streaked with white, although he was still a young man. Perhaps it was because of what was happening. Most of the joy that the people had felt when the mandate was announced began to disappear. Sir Herbert Samuel, in whom so many Jews had had so much faith, appointed a council to help him run the country. Although there were seventeen members, only three were Jews. The rest were Arabs and British.

"Is this the way they prepare us to govern ourselves?" the people of Tel Aviv and Jerusalem asked each other.

"Why is he so unsympathetic to us?"

"And what about Article Six of the mandate?"

Article Six said Britain should help Jews to go to Palestine, but no Jew could enter there anymore without a certificate, and the British Government was not giving out many certificates.

Many people blamed Sir Herbert.

"Imagine a Jew, one of our own, doing this to us," they said.

Weizmann went to see the British Colonial Secretary in London, but the Secretary told him:

"There is no room to swing a cat in Palestine anymore. It is full. Nobody can enter. What is the use of asking me for certificates?"

This was 1929 and Britain was trying to calm the Arabs by making it harder for Jews to go to Palestine. The Arabs were afraid that if too many Jews came they would be shoved out. They resented many of the immigrants, who talked and dressed and behaved differently from any people in the Middle East. They were suspicious of the hospitals these Jews from Europe set up. They did not understand the new methods of agriculture they were trying to use. In their ignorance and their fear, the Arabs were unable to see that their own lives might benefit by contact with the Jewish immigrants.

Ben-Gurion saw his people treated unfairly wherever he looked. Most of the men who worked for the British Government were armed—except the Jews. For Jewish laborers all was not well either. It was hard for them to get jobs because Arabs would work for less money. Tel Aviv was growing like a bed of mushrooms after a summer rain. "But within the rising walls of this Jewish city," Ben-Gurion said, "you rarely hear a Hebrew phrase or melody. Arab labor is doing the work."

The year 1929 ended with bloodshed in Jerusalem. For two hours hot-tempered Arabs attacked Jews and stole their property. The British sent a study commission to find out what had happened, then issued an official government statement known as a White Paper. It said that only a few Jews each year could go to Palestine or buy land there. This made all the Jews of Palestine unhappy, but especially Ben-Gurion, because the Prime Minister of England at this time was Ramsay MacDonald, and Ben-Gurion had always thought of him as a friend of the Jewish people.

Soon afterward in Jerusalem a happy event took place. A baby girl was born to Paula and Ben-Gurion, and she was named Renana, which means rejoicing. At last Ben-Gurion had a *sabra*, a child born in Israel.

During the next few years Ben-Gurion was away from home most of the time, on business, making speeches, traveling. By 1933 he was the head of a new political party, called Mapai. They made up the name from the first letter of each of the Hebrew words: Party of Palestine Workers. About two years later he became chairman of the Jewish Agency, which was almost like being a Prime Minister.

One of his Arab friends was Musa Alami, a very wise man. He had been to school in Europe, and later was Attorney General of Palestine. He lived in Jerusalem, and it was there one day in the spring of 1936 that he and Ben-Gurion began to meet. They hoped they would be able to work out a plan so that the Arabs and the Jews would each have a country of their own in Palestine.

It was dangerous for both of them, but especially for Musa Alami. Any Arab who was thought to be dealing with Jews might be dragged from his bed and killed.

While Ben-Gurion and Musa Alami were having their second meeting, Arab riots began. First in Jaffa. Then every place where there were Arabs and Jews. The list of dead grew every day.

The Arabs stopped working and went on strike. Soon the whole country was almost paralyzed.

The British Government sent in soldiers from Egypt. Then more soldiers from the island of Malta. Then a whole division from England. And finally another commission to study the reason for the riots.

The men who came from Great Britain to look into the Arab riots were called the Peel Commission, after Lord Peel, their chairman. The report they wrote for their government was four hundred pages long. Ben-Gurion read every word and then went to London and sat in the balcony of the House of Commons, listening to the members discuss the report.

Someone asked him later what he had learned from listening to the discussion, and he said:

"You can do many things with an Englishman but you cannot change him into a non-Englishman. The Englishman does not see things through Jewish eyes, he does not feel things with a Jewish heart, and he does not reason with a Jewish brain."

The Peel Commission wanted to divide Palestine into free Jewish and Arab states, but Britain would still keep Jerusalem and some other cities. The Arabs would get about three-fourths of the land that was left and the Jews would get one-fourth.

In the summer of 1937 the leading Zionists of the world met to talk about the Peel plan for dividing Palestine. There were many bitter arguments.

The American Jews thought it was a poor bargain. Ben-Gurion was for the plan, because, he said: "The best mandatory government in the world is not to be compared with a government of our own." He believed this was a beginning and the Jews should not refuse it.

Finally the members of the meeting made a decision that saved everyone's face but settled nothing. They decided to find out more about the British plan for Palestine before doing anything else.

Ben-Gurion was then fifty years old, but more than ever his goal in life was to rebuild the nation of Israel. Everything he did from then on would be to this end.

CHAPTER SEVEN

Arab attacks against the Jews had gone on for more than two years, and there was no sign of the end.

Bands of armed men roamed the country killing Jews. Trains were derailed. Mines were planted in the roads. Telephone wires were torn from their poles. Fruit trees were ripped up by the roots. Travelers were robbed and trucks were held up.

Everyone knew that the Palestinian Arabs were being given money and arms by their Arab neighbors in Egypt, Jordan, Syria, and Lebanon. These were nervous days and sleepless nights for the Jews of Palestine. Each night they would take turns doing guard duty outside their homes and in their streets.

Paula was one of them. "Night after night I would put the children to bed and go out and do the night watch" she said. "I would return during the early hours of the morning before the children woke up."

One day in 1938 the newspapers told how Adolf

Hitler the Nazi dictator of Germany had taken over Austria, and then from Germany came the news that hundreds of synagogues and Jewish apartment buildings had been set afire. Thousands of Jews were arrested in Germany and thousands more in Austria. Many Jewish shops were robbed, and all Jews had to wear the yellow Star of David as identification. Antisemitism was official German policy.

Ben-Gurion asked the British Colonial Office if a hundred thousand Jews who had been facing death in Europe could come into Israel. The Colonial Office said no.

The Jews of Palestine were bitter. They did not know where to turn. They wanted a leader, someone to show them the way out of their troubles.

Weizmann could not do it, for he was the one who had been telling them that they must always trust the British.

But Jabotinsky had an answer. He formed a secret army and called it in Hebrew, *Irgun Zvai Leumi*, the National Military Organization, and it was known as The Irgun or by its initials IZL which were pronounced "Etzel." It was an army of terrorism. He and his men decided that for every Jew the British hurt, the Irgun would hurt three of them. For every Jew the Arabs killed, the Irgun would kill three of them.

There were many in Palestine, especially young people, who wanted to strike back at the Arabs and the British, so Jabotinsky's army became very popular. But there were others who wanted to settle things in a peaceful way, among them Ben-Gurion. He was opposed to terrorism and killing . He said, "It is a sin to spill innocent blood.... When we explain that the Bible commands us not to kill, nobody listens...."

He called on them to be brave.

"Are we scared because Jews are murdered every day?" he asked them. "Jews have been killed ever since resettlement began sixty years ago. Did this frighten us away? What is wrong for Arabs is wrong for Jews .... The Arabs, too, have their patriotic excuses. They do not murder just for fun."

He ended by telling them: "We are a small people, with no army, no state.... We cannot overawe the world. Our strength lies in.... the moral purity of our lives and works.... Given courage, understanding, and clean hands, we shall win."

In Palestine that night a great many Jews who had been troubled slept better.

But Ben-Gurion still had to decide whether he should help Jews from Europe come into Palestine illegally. At first he was against it because he thought it would make the British angry if they found out. Then they might refuse to give out any more certificates legally admitting Jews to Palestine.

In the meantime many Jews were smuggled into the country by Jabotinsky and the Irgun, past the British ships that were guarding the ports.

Then slowly Ben-Gurion changed his mind. He had lost hope of persuading the British to give him more certificates. So finally he allowed Haganah, the underground army, to form a Committee for Illegal Immigration. Its headquarters were in Paris, and before long its agents were scattered all over Europe. The Jews who were going to Palestine this way always went on board the ships at night, and the ships were always in communication by radio with Haganah in Palestine. Haganah would direct them to lonely spots along the Palestine shore. When they arrived, men and girls from Haganah helped them ashore and hid them before the British could sound an alarm.

Several months later, in the spring of 1939, the British Government issued another White Paper, called Command 6019. It said that fifteen thousand Jews could come into Palestine each year for five years. After that, not a single Jew would ever be admitted unless the Arabs agreed. Jews would not be allowed to buy land except in certain parts of Palestine, and the British Government would help the Arabs to form an independent nation in Palestine.

Command 6019 killed the hopes of millions of Jews in Europe. It violated the Mandate for Palestine given in 1920 at San Remo to Great Britain.

In Tel Aviv and Jerusalem there were demonstrations by angry Jews against it that quickly turned into riots.

CHAPTER EIGHT

About a week after World War II started, Ben-Gurion met secretly with the officers of the Haganah underground army. He told them that, in spite of the war and the rules the British had made against them, Jewish immigrants would keep coming to Palestine. But he also told them they should help the British win the war against the Nazis. There was hardly a Jewish family in Palestine that did not have relatives in Europe whom the Nazis had killed or robbed. Ben-Gurion said they should ask for volunteers who wanted to help the British.

In a short time more than a hundred thousand Jewish men and women had joined up.

Soon after this, Ben-Gurion packed a suitcase, took some of his favorite books under his arm, and set off for England.

"I must help Weizmann get a Jewish Legion for us," he told his wife. "I'll be back as soon as I can."

By this time Paula was used to his long absences,

but she worried about him. Sometimes he had dark rings under his eyes because he got so little sleep.

When he was in Palestine, she could see that he ate good food and could keep people from bothering him when he should be sleeping. But when he went away she knew what happened, because once she had gone along on a trip. Other men who had the same dream for the Jews would keep him awake half the night talking. He would never think of eating unless someone reminded him.

Now he was off to London, where the people were getting ready for the attacks they were sure the German planes would make on their city.

But though she was worried, all Paula said to her husband was:

"Take care of yourself, won't you?"

Then he was gone.

Ben-Gurion found a small room in a boarding-house in London. It was several miles by Underground railway to Great Russell Street and the yellow building that housed the Jewish Agency, where Ben-Gurion was given a small, bare office on the second floor. From the window he could see the rooftops of Bloomsbury and two flowering trees in Montague Street.

Often he would sit in his small office with his eyes closed, just thinking. He kept to himself more than ever before, and he would be silent for long periods.

Once when there was an air raid and everyone else had gone to a shelter, someone asked:

"Where's Ben-Gurion?"

An hour after the raid was over, he calmly walked into the building. When they asked him where he had been, he said he had been to a movie.

"That one at the top of Tottenham Court Road."

What was the picture? they asked him.

He didn't know, he said. He had had his eyes closed.

They didn't understand him at all. Why did he sit in a theater with his eyes closed? they asked.

Because the seats were comfortable, it didn't cost much, and it was such a good place to think, he answered.

Several months after Ben-Gurion arrived in London, German planes began to come over the city every day, dropping bombs.

One day when he had to spend several hours in an air-raid shelter he turned to the man next to him and said:

"If I have to do this, I'm going to use the time to study ancient Greek."

"Why Greek?" the man asked.

"The future of Israel may depend upon our knowing something about military matters."

"And what does this have to do with Greek?"

"I want to read Thucydides, the great Greek historian, on military strategy," Ben-Gurion answered.

The sky was often noisy with German planes, and there was death above in the streets, but David Ben-Gurion taught himself Greek in the air-raid shelters in London in 1940.

At his desk in the yellow building on Great Russell Street he worked on a plan to help the British win the war, to save as many Jews as possible from the Nazis, and to prepare for the building of a Jewish nation in Palestine after the war was over.

When he had finished working out his plan, he and Weizmann took it to the Colonial Office.

The Colonial Secretary asked them:

"If you are really interested in a British victory, why don't your people just enlist in the British Army?"

Ben-Gurion snapped back:

"Why don't you ask this of the French or the Czechs or the Poles?"

Then the Secretary said that a Jewish Legion would "just increase our troubles out there." But he added that if Weizmann and Ben-Gurion really wanted to help Britain they should go at once to the United States and ask the Jews there to persuade the American Government to enter the war on Britain's side.

Weizmann was working as a chemist for the British Government, so he could not go. But Ben-Gurion packed his bag, put a Greek dictionary in his coat pocket, and headed for New York.

CHAPTER NINE

In New York, Ben-Gurion moved into a plain hotel and started to work.

Paula's sister and her children wanted to give dinner parties for him. Other people wanted him to go to the theater. But he was too busy meeting with important Americans who could help his people in Palestine.

He had long talks with Rabbi Stephen Wise, a prominent American Zionist, and U.S. Supreme Court Justice Louis D. Brandeis. He addressed a big meeting in Carnegie Hall and denounced the White Paper. He spoke to leaders of Hadassah, the organization of American Jewish women who were Zionists.

After three months he was off again. They wanted him back in Palestine. Paula was very glad to see him return. She had been worrying about him.

By now Amos Ben-Gurion was a young man and had joined the British Army. Geula was married. Of the three children, only Renana was still at home.

Jabotinsky had died in 1940, but his secret Jewish army, the Irgun, was still active, and a man named Abraham Stern had formed a new band called Fighters for The Freedom of Israel, but known as the Stern Gang. They were even more extreme than Irgun, for they did not stop at attacking the Arabs and the British. One day, to get money, they stole twenty thousand dollars from a bank in Tel Aviv. The bank was owned by the Jews, and everyone knew it, but the Stern Gang needed money for its terrorist activities.

Palestine was a very busy place. There were British troops everywhere. Jewish factories were working overtime to turn out war material for the British—everything from hospital beds to ships. Jewish scientists were making drugs that were badly needed.

Soon after the British and American troops had landed in France in 1944, Winston Churchill, the Prime Minister of England, said: "The government has decided to accede to the request of the Jewish Agency for Palestine that a Jewish Brigade group should be formed to take part in active operations...."

At last, more than four years after the war began, the Jews could go into a Jewish unit if they wished, and wear proudly on their shoulders a patch with the Star of David, that star Hitler forced the Jews of Germany to wear as a mark of their shame. Now it was a badge of courage and honor.

CHAPTER TEN

Everyone alive then remembers something about 1945. The events of that year changed the life of almost everyone in the world.

In 1945, President Franklin D. Roosevelt of the United States died. Hitler killed himself. Mussolini, the fascist dictator of Italy and Hitler's partner, was captured and killed. The first atom bombs were exploded. The war in Europe ended with the Nazis' complete defeat. The United Nations was formed. Japan surrendered.

For Ben-Gurion, 1945 was a year to remember for other reasons.

In March, seven Arab countries—Egypt, Lebanon, Jordan, Syria, Iraq, Saudi Arabia, and Yemen— formed the Arab League. One of the aims of the League was to drive the Jews out of Palestine.

In May came good news: Germany had surrendered. There was dancing in the streets of every city in Palestine and in the *kibbutzim*, which was the Hebrew name for the farm settlements.

As usual, Ben-Gurion was calm while others celebrated, for, he said:

"Europe is liberated, but who can guarantee that what happened once cannot happen again?"

In June he went to New York to see Rudolf G. Sonneborn, a wealthy businessman who wanted to help him build a state for the Jewish people. Seventeen of Sonneborn's friends and business associates came to his home to meet Ben-Gurion. It was Sunday, the first of July, and a blistering hot day. At ten o'clock in the morning the men gathered in the large living room. Ben-Gurion stood by a grand piano as he talked. A luncheon had been laid out at the end of the room, but nobody ate anything. Some of the men who sat listening sipped cool drinks. Ben-Gurion himself had his shirt open at the neck and the perspiration was streaming down his face, but he talked to the men for three hours. Then they began to ask him questions.

Twilight came and they were still talking. But Ben-Gurion's sincerity won them over. Every man promised to help as much as he could, and also promised not to say a word about it. Their code name would be "the Sonneborn Institute," and Ben-Gurion would find some way to communicate with them when the time was right. Secrecy would be necessary, because the Sonneborn Institute was going to buy ships to smuggle Jews into Palestine and buy arms and perhaps even war planes. Ben-Gurion went back to Palestine, confident that his New York friends would help him.

A few weeks later Great Britain held its first general elections since the war, and the Labour party won.

Before the elections the leaders of the Labour party said they were in favor of moving the Arabs out of Palestine, letting all Jews come in who wanted to, and making the whole place a Jewish state. This was more than Ben-Gurion or anyone else had even asked for.

On the night of July 26 the Jews of Palestine went wild as they listened on their radios to the results of the British election.

While they celebrated, Ben-Gurion went to his study quietly and wrote:

"The war is over now, and nobody can expect us any longer to tolerate the White Paper."

In August, President Truman received a report from Earl Harrison, an emissary he had sent to Europe. It said that a hundred thousand Jewish survivors of Hitler's death camps were living in dirty, crowded sites in various parts of Europe and had no place to go. Many of them were sick, and they had no way of earning a living. So the President sent a message to Clement Attlee, the new Prime Minister of Great

Ben-Gurion in the uniform of the Royal Fusiliers during World War One. Ben-Gurion worked diligently to establish a Jewish brigade to serve on the side of the Allies during the war. *(Israel State Archives)*

This farewell assembly at Ben-Gurion's home in Plonsk, Poland, 1906, given in honor of Ben-Gurion who sits in the center of the first row. See the "X" on his white shirt. A few days later he and Rachel Nelkin Bit-Halachmi (to Ben-Gurion's left) and Shlomo Zemach (to Rachel's left) departed for Palestine. *(Israel State Archives)*

Ben-Gurion and his bride, Paula. Photo taken shortly after they were married in New York in 1918. *(Consulate General of Israel)*

During the 1930's Ben-Gurion met frequently with Palestine Arab leaders to discuss matters of mutual concern in the hopes that the conflict between the two communities, Arab and Jewish, could be resolved peacefully. *(Israel State Archives)*

David Ben-Guiron and his friend, Yitzhak Ben-Zvi in Constantinople.
(Israel State Archives)

The Ben-Gurion family in the early 1930's. *(Israel State Archives)*

On May 14, 1948, the leaders of the Yishuv gathered in Tel Aviv to proclaim the birth of the State of Israel. The meeting began with the singing of *Hatikvah*. The leaders of what become Israel's Provisional Parliament stand beneath a portrait of Theodor Herzl. This is most fitting as this meeting fulfilled his prophecy. *(Israel State Archives)*

Just before rising to read Israel's Declaration of Independence, Ben-Gurion mops his brow. *(Israel State Archives)*

Ben-Gurion waits for silence before reading the Declaration of Independence. *(Israel State Archives)*

The newly elected first President of Israel, Dr. Chaim Weizmann, is introduced to Israel's Parliament for the first time by Prime Minister David Ben-Gurion. *(Israel State Archives)*

Ben-Gurion needed eyeglasses for close work, but he rarely was photographed wearing them. In this unique photograph he is seen at his desk with his glasses on. *(Israel State Archives)*

Upon his return from his first trip to the United States as Prime Minister, hundreds of thousands of Israeli citizens filled the streets of Tel Aviv to welcome Ben-Gurion home. *(Israel State Archives)*

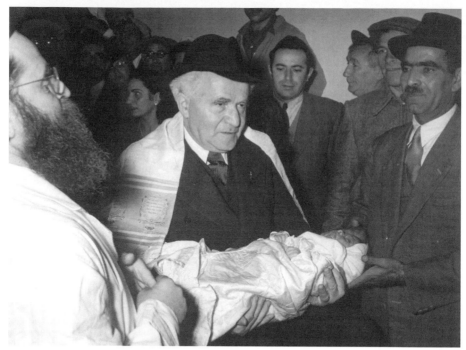

Prime Minister Ben-Gurion, who always enjoyed participating in the ceremony of *brit milah*, attended this day and is seen holding the newborn child. *(Israel State Archives)*

Ben-Gurion meets members of the village of Patish after an Arab guerrilla attack. Ben-Gurion was determined to keep the borders of Israel free of such outrages, and was vigilant in visiting all areas of the new country subjected to these attacks. *(Israel State Archives)*

Britain, who was also the head of the Labour party. He suggested to Mr. Attlee that the hundred thousand Jews be allowed to go to Palestine as quickly as possible.

Soon afterward Zionists from all over the world had a meeting in London again. The new British Foreign Secretary, Ernest Bevin, had said nothing about the Jews in Palestine yet, but most of the people at the meeting were still hopeful. Ben-Gurion was not. He told them they had better be ready for a shock.

The shock came one day when Ben-Gurion was called to the Colonial Office. There he was given a copy of a speech the Foreign Secretary, Mr. Bevin, would be reading to the House of Commons in a half hour.

Ben-Gurion quickly went back to the Jewish Agency building on Great Russell Street. Weizmann was waiting for him there, and together they read the speech. It was even worse than Ben-Gurion had predicted it would be. The promises of the Labour party had meant nothing. Instead of saving a hundred thousand Jews, instead of admitting all Jews who wished to come to Palestine, Bevin was going to let them bring in only fifteen hundred a month, and no more. He told the Jews to stay in Europe, to build new lives next to the graves of their families.

Instead of a Jewish state, they were going to get another commission. Then another report. More words, and words, and words.

Weizmann walked silently from the room. His shoulders sagged, and he looked much older. But Ben-Gurion would not admit defeat. He had a plan.

Several days later Rudolf Sonneborn in New York received a telephone call from a man who said he had a message from Ben-Gurion. He would not tell Sonneborn who he was; he just gave him the message:

"The time has come!"

So the Sonneborn Institute, the seventeen men who had come to Sonneborn's apartment that hot July Sunday, and some of their trusted friends, bought more than a dozen ships that were needed to bring Jews to their ancient homeland. They also bought planes and guns and other war material. These were stored in many different countries of the world until they would be needed, for the time had come for the Jews to fight for their homeland.

CHAPTER ELEVEN

When Bevin read his speech to the British House of Commons, Jewish leaders in Palestine decided to call a protest strike the next day. Everyone stopped work, and meetings were held peacefully in the cities.

But that night, some Jewish terrorists went on a rampage. They broke into British Government offices in Tel Aviv, smashed furniture, destroyed valuable papers, and even set fires.

Jewish and British policemen tried to stop them, but they failed. Finally British soldiers came and opened fire, killing several Jews. Then a curfew was put on the country. No one would be allowed on the streets at night.

During the next ten days there was more rioting and shooting. Many Jewish children were killed and wounded.

Sometime later a committee of British and American experts appointed by both governments arrived in Palestine to study what to do with Palestine and with the hundreds of thousands of European Jews who sought to go there. It was called the Anglo-American Committee of Inquiry, with twelve members, six Americans, six British.

They came to Palestine from Egypt via a train ride from Cairo that had taken twelve hours. Jerusalem looked to them more like an army camp than a holy city. All the important buildings were surrounded by barbed wire. There were pillboxes at the entrance to the King David Hotel, where they were going to stay. They could see tanks down the side streets and soldiers with guns on the rooftops of the buildings.

The hotel itself was filled with Arab sheiks in white robes, private detectives, Zionists, newspaper reporters, and British army officers.

Ben-Gurion was asked to come to a committee meeting to answer some questions. By this time he was used to it. This was the eighteenth committee that had come to Palestine.

While he was at the meeting, Ben-Gurion asked the committee a few questions of his own:

"Why is there this discrimination against us? Jews are not the only people who are different from others. In truth they are not different at all....

"We are what we are, and we like to be what we are. Is that a crime?..."

He turned to the American members of the committee and said:

"More than three hundred years ago a ship by the name of *Mayflower* left Plymouth for the New World. It was a great event in American and English history. I wonder how many Englishmen and how many Americans know exactly the date when that ship left Plymouth, and how many people were on that ship, and what was the kind of bread those people ate when they left Plymouth?"

Some of the Americans smiled, and some shook their heads.

Then Ben-Gurion said, "Well, more than thirty-three hundred years ago the Jews left Egypt. It was three thousand years before the *Mayflower*. But every Jew in the world knows the exact date. It was the fifteenth of Nisan. The bread they ate was *matzoh*.

"Up until today all the Jews in the world, in America, in Russia, everywhere, on the fifteenth of Nisan eat the same *matzoh* and tell the story of the exile to Egypt.... They finish with these two sentences:

"'This year we are slaves, next year we shall be free. This year we are here, next year we shall be in the land of Israel.'"

Amos Ben-Gurion had joined the Jewish Brigade and gone through many battles during the war without being wounded, but just after the war ended he had to go to a hospital in Liverpool, England, because he had become sick. His nurse was Mary Cal-

low. Mary was a pretty English girl with dark hair.
Before long Amos wrote his mother and father that
he was in love. There was only one problem: she was
not Jewish. But she had agreed to change her religion.

Soon after he received this news, Amos's father
had to leave on another trip to Europe. As he packed
his suitcase he slipped in some books from his library
that he thought Mary should read.

He was two hours late for the wedding, but when
he met his daughter-in-law he was very pleased with
her. Still he was a little worried.

"Do you realize what this is going to mean?" he
asked her. "It will be you who will have to make the
sacrifice, not Amos—living in a strange land, among
people who talk a language you do not yet understand, and—"

She tried to stop him, but he went on.

"Are you sure you are ready to make such a sacrifice?"

She assured him she was, so he smiled and gave
her the books he had brought her.

Ben-Gurion was in Paris when the report of the
Anglo-American Committee was announced. "We must
flatly reject it!" he said when he had read it. The
committee agreed with President Truman that a hundred thousand Jews should be allowed to go to Pal-

estine at once. But the members did not think there should be a Jewish state.

Instead the United Nations should run the country until it could be made into a state that would be governed by Jews and Arabs equally.

People were secretly coming into Palestine by the thousands. While Jewish underground workers were trying to get them ashore and hide them, they often fought with the British troops. Almost every night trains and bridges were blown up.

The trouble became worse, until the British decided to put an end to it once and for all. One Sabbath morning many people in Palestine were awakened by the noise of gunfire. British sound trucks moved through the streets of the cities, bellowing the news that another curfew had been put on the country.

"No one is to move from where he is at this moment!" the voice said.

Those who turned on their radios heard the explanation. It was being announced that the British High Commissioner in Palestine had begun "military operations" against the Jewish Agency and Haganah because they were blamed for all the trouble.

In Jerusalem, British soldiers took over Jewish Agency headquarters, dynamited their way into other Jewish offices that were locked because it was the Sabbath, and began to round up the Jewish leaders.

Dr. Weizmann was about to go to London for an eye operation, and the British ignored him.

The head of Haganah slipped by the British and went into hiding. Ben-Gurion and a colleague, Reuven Shiloah, were still in Paris. Most of the other important members of the Agency were seized and taken to a prison camp.

Ben-Gurion received the bad news in a cable sent to him from Jerusalem. It was in code and warned him that neither he nor Shiloah should return to Palestine then because they would be arrested.

"I must go at once," Ben-Gurion kept saying.

Shiloah urged him to be patient.

"But if there is danger, I must be there!" Ben-Gurion insisted.

Shiloah kept telling him that he would be of much more use to his people if he stayed out of prison.

Ben-Gurion had to agree, but for days he walked back and forth in his hotel room. He jumped every time the phone rang, and he nervously read all of the newspaper stories.

Soon afterward, on a hot night in July, some friends came to tell him frightening news. It had been announced on the radio that the King David Hotel in Jerusalem had been blown up. A hundred people might be dead.

Ben-Gurion spent hours near a radio. This was terrible, and he knew it undoubtedly was the work of Irgun, the terrorist organization led now by

Menachem Begin that thought bombings and killings would frighten the British into leaving Palestine.

Two days later the British Government issued a White Paper. It said that for many months Irgun and the Stern Gang had been working with Haganah, and Haganah was controlled by the Jewish Agency. Therefore Ben-Gurion was responsible for the bombing of the King David Hotel, for he was the head of the Agency.

Actually Ben-Gurion knew nothing about the plans to bomb the hotel, and to make this clear to everyone he set these words down on paper in his own hand:

"We do not control the terrorists. We wield no influence over them and we need bear no sort of responsibility... for their actions. They have flouted every form of national and communal discipline."

Soon afterward Ben-Gurion sailed for the United States, since he still could not go back to Palestine without being arrested. He answered some questions at a United Nations meeting in New York and he went to Washington, D.C., to find out if America had any plans to help the Jews in Palestine.

When he returned to New York, a group of reporters were waiting to interview him. After the interview was over, a young woman reporter offered to show him what she had written about him before she gave it to her paper. She was very proud of her story. It began:

"There is a man in our town tonight who is to the little people of Palestine what Abraham Lincoln was to the people of America in his day."

Ben-Gurion read the words twice and grunted angrily.

"How dare you compare me with Abraham Lincoln?" he asked.

The young woman tried to explain, but Ben-Gurion interrupted her.

His anger was gone now, and he said quietly:

"When I think of a great man, I think of Abraham Lincoln. Who am I? Just a little Jew."

CHAPTER TWELVE

Ben-Gurion tried once more in 1947 to work out everything peacefully with the British. He went to London and saw Ernest Bevin, Britain's Foreign Secretary.

Bevin showed no interest in Ben-Gurion's dream of reviving the splendor of ancient Israel, but he finally suggested that a committee from the United Nations be chosen to govern Palestine. Both the Jews and the Arabs refused this plan.

So Ben-Gurion went home. At last the warrant for his arrest had been torn up.

He had been away almost a year. He found Paula and his daughters, Geula and Renana, well, but tired, as most of the people in Tel Aviv were.

While he had been away, he had had a birthday, his sixtieth. But he didn't celebrate it; he did not believe in celebrating birthdays.

"What is there to celebrate?" he said. "You didn't

have anything to, do with your own birth. If you want to celebrate, do it on the anniversary of a day on which *you* did something; something important, like settling in Palestine."

Now he had to prepare for war. Despite his age he was going to teach himself what a supreme commander should know about running an army. He read all the books he could find on military science. One by one, he called the leaders of Haganah to his home and took them to his library. There he asked them many questions about military matters.

First, Yaacov Dostrovsky, Haganah's chief of staff. Then Israel Galili, a young farmer who was also a Haganah commander.

Then Yigael Yadin. His father was a famous archaeologist, and Yigael was following in his father's path. He and Ben-Gurion had long arguments, and sometimes Ben-Gurion would pound the table until the glasses rattled and occasionally bounced off onto the floor. At times like these others might have said, "Yes, Ben-Gurion," but not Yadin. He was slim and almost a foot taller than his chief, and he said what he thought, but Ben-Gurion liked him for it.

Then, Yigal Allon, a sandy-haired young *sabra*. He was a tough-talking soldier, a commander of Palmach, the commando outfit.

Ben-Gurion called these men by their first names, and they called him "Ben-Gurion" to his face and "the Old Man" or "BG" when he was not there. He would sit with a notebook on his knees, a pencil in his hand, writing hundreds of pages on what they told him.

Then he left his library and began to travel about the country, visiting Haganah camps. "What do we need most?" he kept asking.

Haganah had fifty thousand soldiers, an artillery unit with no artillery, an Air Force with six old planes hidden in a *kibbutz*, and a few British planes that could be used to drop supplies to settlements or as bombers. It had ten thousand rifles and a few hundred machine guns, mortars, and homemade Sten guns, but no tanks, no flame throwers, nor other modern weapons.

The soldiers had no uniforms. They wore khaki shirts and khaki shorts, but many other people did also, because they were the cheapest and most practical clothing for Palestine.

There were no badges of rank and no patches to tell one unit of the Army from another.

Ben-Gurion had a feeling that the day would soon come when the Jews of Palestine would have to fight for the right to have a country. He estimated that they had only a few months to turn this band of amateurs into a real army, so he gave most of his time and thought to the task. Paula and his daughters seldom saw him during these days.

In April of 1947 there was a United Nations meeting about Palestine, and the U.N. decided to appoint a committee of eleven men to go there. It was known as UNSCOP, pronounced as a single word. It was an abbreviation for the United Nations Special Committee on Palestine. Some of the members had an idea: to divide the country between Arabs and Jews. When they asked Ben-Gurion his opinion, he said to them:

"We feel we are entitled to Palestine as a whole, but we will be ready to consider the matter of a Jewish state in an adequate area of Palestine."

The committee members leaned forward.

"Then you are not opposed to partition?" one of them asked.

"We are ready to consider it," Ben-Gurion replied.

The U.N. committee reported that the British must leave Palestine. Most of them agreed with Ben-Gurion that there should be partition of Palestine—an Arab and a Jewish state.

Britain answered that she was ready to leave Palestine, whether she was forced out or not.

In November the United Nations Assembly voted for the partition plan and ordered Great Britain to leave Palestine in eight months. A Jewish and an Arab state would be set up two months after that. The Land of Israel was to be divided and shared.

Ben-Gurion was in the north of Palestine when the news came. He rushed back to Jerusalem. From the windows of the Jewish Agency building he watched the crowds beginning to form in King George V Road. At last they really had something to celebrate. They danced the *hora* and waved their blue-and-white flags and sang *Hatikvah*, but Ben-Gurion went to his desk and began to write:

"Even after the Jewish state is established, we dare not delude ourselves that all our troubles will have been resolved and that henceforth life will be all joy and festivity."

CHAPTER THIRTEEN

During the next six months it seemed to Ben-Gurion that almost everything and everybody had turned against the *Yishuv*.

First there were the forty million Arabs in the neighboring countries. He had been warning everyone that they would probably attack as soon as the Jewish state was set up.

Then there were the Arabs inside Palestine. Bands of them roamed the countryside, killing and robbing people, and they attacked trucks carrying Jewish settlers to the *kibbutzim* in the desert.

In Haifa suddenly the Arab military commander announced that all the Arabs in the city would become refugees of their own free will. Haganah sound trucks rode all over Haifa, broadcasting a message from Ben-Gurion to the Arabs. He asked them to stay and promised they would be treated fairly in the new Jewish state. But their leaders had ordered them to leave, so they left.

Then there were the British. They upset everybody's plans by saying they would leave Palestine on May 15, instead of later, as had been decided by the U.N.

Jerusalem was a great problem. This city was the center of all Jewish history. It should have been the center of the new Jewish state, but the United Nations had decided that the Jews' holy city was to belong not to them but to everyone. It was to be an international city.

Love of Jerusalem was in every part of Ben-Gurion's being. So when one of his military advisers said they should withdraw from the city, he shook his head.

"How will you supply it?" the adviser asked.

"We will find a way!" Ben-Gurion answered.

"How will you defend it?"

"I believe in miracles," said Ben-Gurion.

The Irgun was also causing trouble. During a combined Irgun-Haganah attempt to clear the road from Tel Aviv to Jerusalem, members of the terrorist organization killed more than two hundred Arab men, women, and children in the Arab village of Deir Yassin. The Arab leaders of the village said the killings had been brutal and unnecessary.

Ben-Gurion was very angry that Jews would do such a terrible thing, and immediately he sent a message to the King Abdullah of Transjordan saying he was sorry and that the men of Irgun had not done this on his orders.

He was tired now, but this was no time to think about himself. Paula tried to take care of him. She insisted that he eat nourishing food and she watched over him when he slept, so that neither people nor noises would disturb him. But Ben-Gurion saw little of his home, his wife, his daughters, or his books in those days.

Chief of Staff Dostrovsky was too sick to come to his office, so he had to do his part of planning the war from his home.

Yigael Yadin was taking Dostrovsky's place in Tel Aviv, and he came every day to talk to Ben-Gurion at his office. Together they spent hours looking at maps and making plans.

Others came with questions about telephones, the water supply, the immigrants, and taxes. Sometimes there seemed no end to the problems of building a new country.

One day the man in charge of the post office came and asked Ben-Gurion if he wouldn't, please, do something about getting a name for the new country. He wanted to order postage stamps, but how could he even talk with the artist who would make the design unless he knew what the name of the country was going to be?

Ben-Gurion waved him away. There was no time

to talk about such things. So the first stamps had only the words *Doar Ivri*—the Jewish Postal Service.

Ben-Gurion was much more concerned about something else. He told his colleagues:

"When the time comes, there will be enough men who will eagerly make themselves available for positions of importance in the government. What worries me is the public services—locomotive drivers to run our trains, operators to man our telephone exchanges—the hospitals."

So he decided that a committee called a Provisional Council would be appointed. Each man on the committee was to make a plan for running a certain number of government departments, and all these plans were to be used as soon as the mandate ended and they were free.

One day the committee met to choose the place where the government would be located until they could build new offices. They chose Sarona, a settlement of stone farmhouses on the edge of Tel Aviv, and they renamed it Hakirya—The City.

One by one or in twos and threes the men of the committee went to Hakirya to look at the houses and decide which department would use which farmhouse, and whose secretary would be in which kitchen, and whether the wine cellars would be good air-raid shelters. Desks and chairs and filing cabinets had to be made and stored somewhere in preparation for the big day.

Then Ben-Gurion and his future Cabinet made an announcement. A Jewish state would be declared, they told the world. It would be born the moment the mandate ended.

These days Ben-Gurion was everywhere. He visited the secret war plants and inspected the front lines of the Army, giving words of encouragement to the men. He issued orders to Haganah's officers that if war came they must plan their campaign so that as few of their men as possible would be killed or wounded. Haganah had no soldiers to spare. Besides, Ben-Gurion hated the necessity of sacrificing lives. At the same time he would not let them desert any of the settlements, even if they were hard to defend, because each settlement was valuable to this primitive country. He told them:

"We shall fight for each Jewish spot, foot by foot, house by house."

When they heard this, some people became angry and said he was being stubborn, but many more were inspired to fight bravely.

As the big day drew near, with everyone more excited than ever before, a policeman appeared one morning at a chemical laboratory in Tel Aviv. He was holding a plate with a pat of butter on it. In the hall the girl at the desk looked at the butter and then at the policeman.

"It's to be analyzed," he explained.

"Analyzed for what?" he asked the policeman.

"For Paula Ben-Gurion," the policeman replied.

The girl called a chemist.

The chemist smiled and telephoned Mrs. Ben-Gurion.

"I want it analyzed because I think the place it came from is cheating my David and sending him poor quality butter," she said. "He's a busy man these days, and he must have the best food there is, to keep him going. You analyze it and tell me the truth."

CHAPTER FOURTEEN

The British said they would give up their mandate and start leaving at midnight on Friday, May 14.

On Wednesday morning of that week Ben-Gurion called the Provisional Council to a meeting. The most important question was whether most of them still agreed this was the time to declare the state. Ben-Gurion wanted no one to say, later, that he alone had made the decision or shouted down the people who were against it.

Yigael Yadin told them he had learned that the armies of all the surrounding Arab states were moving toward the Arab areas of Palestine. They could expect an attack from all directions on Saturday and air raids on Tel Aviv.

In spite of this they voted to carry out their plan for a Jewish state.

The next question was to decide the exact time when the state should be declared. It should not be done until midnight of Friday because the mandate would not end until then. But at sundown on Friday the Sabbath would begin, and after that the Orthodox members of the council would not be able to sign their names or travel by automobile.

But they figured out that if they started the declaration ceremony at four o'clock on Friday it would be finished well before the setting of the sun.

After the council meeting ended, a meeting of the future Cabinet was held. One of the things they had to decide on was a name for the new state. Many names were suggested, among them Zion, Judea, and Ever, meaning "Hebrew."

"I suggest Israel," said a voice. It was Ben-Gurion himself who had spoken.

The word sounded strange at first. They kept saying it, half aloud, trying it out.

"Israel."

"The Israeli Government."

"An Israeli citizen."

Most of them knew that the original meaning of Israel is "the one who contested with God" and was originally applied in the Bible to Jacob, whose children were called "the children of Israel."

Ben-Gurion asked them to take a vote. The majority voted for "Israel." So the new country had a name.

On Thursday invitations were sent to about two hundred Jews in Palestine, asking them to be at the Municipal Museum of Tel Aviv at three-thirty in the afternoon on Friday, May 14. They were to wear "festive dark clothes" and to be very sure to keep both the time and the place a secret.

On Friday, the most important day of his life, David Ben-Gurion rose from bed at seven o'clock in the morning, dressed, and went downstairs to the kitchen. He greeted Paula with a few affectionate words of Hebrew and then sat down at the table to have his coffee while he looked at the morning newspapers.

"There was a call that you must be at headquarters for another meeting at nine," she told him.

Outside the house an army jeep was waiting for him.

At headquarters a dozen officers were bending over maps. Ben-Gurion listened to what they said. There was a frown on his face most of the time. He kept opening and closing his fists impatiently.

Messengers came and went. Some of the notes they brought from the commanders at the front lines were good news; some were bad.

At Latrun the enemy's artillery had fired at the Jewish forces all night. The only piece of artillery Haganah had was captured.

Suddenly there was the noise of a plane. Ben-Gurion ran to the window. It was flying low.

"British," someone said.

"It looks as if the British are really leaving," another officer said.

Yadin suggested that Ben-Gurion order the people to make air-raid shelters, dig trenches, and help build road blocks.

The Old Man went to work.

At noon a jeep drove him home. Paula opened the door.

"What news?" she asked.

He told her what had happened since morning and then went into the kitchen to each his lunch— vegetables that Paula had cooked for him. Just as he finished, Amos and his wife, Mary, arrived with their child. Amos was now the commander of a regiment, and he and his father talked about the air raids that might come the next day.

"Why are there no air-raid shelters in Tel Aviv?" Ben-Gurion asked his son. "I have been warning for a long time about the danger of raids, but no one listens. "

Mary asked, "Is it true that we have only one piece of artillery?"

Ben-Gurion smiled when she said "we." She was no longer a stranger; she was one of them now.

"We expect artillery any day," he told her, "and if it does not come we will steal artillery from the enemy."

Then he went to his room to change his clothes. He put on a dark blue suit, a white shirt, dark shoes and socks, and a dark silk tie. Suddenly he called to Paula:

"Has anyone done anything about Rabbi Fishman?"

His old friend, Rabbi Fishman, lived in Jerusalem, which was now partly held by the Arabs. It would be difficult for anyone to get from Jerusalem to Tel Aviv, but Ben-Gurion wanted the rabbi to take part in the ceremony, so a Piper Cub plane was sent for him and he arrived in time.

A messenger came from headquarters. Chief of Staff Dostrovsky had just been taken to the hospital, so Yadin would now have to take over all of his job.

At one o'clock Ben-Gurion had a meeting with the Provisional Council to vote on the name the future Cabinet had chosen for their state, and also on the declaration of independence it had written. When they had voted for both "Israel" and the declaration—with a few changes some of the members wanted-the meeting ended.

As they left the room, Rabbi Fishman stopped Ben-Gurion and asked:

"Are we going to war with the Arabs?"

Ben-Gurion nodded.

"And do we have anything to use in the air against them except that broken-down cart?" he wanted to know.

Then the old rabbi told Ben-Gurion about his trip from Jerusalem.

"A man came to me and said he had orders from the future Prime Minister that I was to come with him. He took me to a field where there was a broken-down old cart."

The rabbi never called the Piper Cub a plane. He insisted it was a broken-down old cart. The pilot tied him in with ropes, and they "flew in twisting ways, sometimes north and sometimes south." He was sure it took a few hours to go the forty air miles.

He kept shaking his head and saying:

"I don't see how we can beat the Arabs with flying carts like that."

Ben-Gurion went home to rest for an hour. As he drove through Tel Aviv the city streets were crowded. People stood in groups, some reading newspapers to learn the latest news about the battle in Jerusalem. The restaurants were packed. Trucks loaded with young soldiers, both men and girls, raced through the streets on their way to the front lines.

Orange juice stands and boys selling flags were doing a good business.

Just before four o'clock a fleet of shining new American automobiles bringing the officials of the new government drew up in front of the Municipal Museum.

The two hundred invited guests had not kept the secret very well, because the street was crowded with people. Many carried blue-and-white flags with the star of David on them. They cheered as each man stepped from a car.

Inside, the future Cabinet members took their

places on the platform. Before them were the members of the Provisional Council, the two chief rabbis of Tel Aviv in tall silk hats, and many reporters and photographers.

Ben-Gurion was the last official to enter the museum. He looked strong and dignified. The reporters started to write in their notebooks.

An artist rushed in with the declaration of independence. He had finished the decoration but not the words. They would have to be put in later. The Tel Aviv Philharmonic Orchestra in the next room played *Hatikvah*, which would be Israel's national anthem.

Then Ben-Gurion stood up to read the declaration. His hand was trembling as he held it. He began:

"The Land of Israel was the birthplace of the Jewish people...

He was trying to keep his voice steady as he went on to say that Israel would be a state based on liberty, justice, and peace. Israel would cooperate with the United Nations and obey its rules. Christian and Moslem holy places would be protected. The hand of peace was held out to Arabs everywhere.

His voice grew stronger. Some of the guests began to choke with tears as they heard Ben-Gurion declare that Israel was now an independent state "on this Sabbath eve, the fifth of Iyar, 5708, the fourteenth day of May 1948."

At exactly 4:37-1/2 in the afternoon Ben-Gurion rapped his gavel and said dramatically:

"I hereby declare this meeting adjourned. The State of Israel has come into being.'

The ceremony was broadcast, and soon throughout the country crowds gathered in the streets and in the restaurants.

When he got home Ben-Gurion said to Paula:

"I feel like the bereaved among the rejoicers."

He was thinking of the soldiers at the battle fronts.

At about the time Ben-Gurion was going to sleep that night, the Haganah secret radio station received a message from America. Yaacov Yanai, head of the Haganah Signal Corps, wrote it down. It asked Ben-Gurion to do a broadcast to the United States.

Yanai called one of Ben-Gurion's aides.

"It's out of the question" said the aide. "The Old Man has gone to bed."

Several hours later the Haganah station heard a news broadcast saying that President Truman had recognized the state of Israel.

This time Yanai drove straight to the Ben-Gurion house and banged on the front door.

Paula finally answered. She was very angry.

"What do you mean by making such a noise?" she said. "You will wake up Ben-Gurion."

Yanai explained what had happened. But Paula

said it made no difference; no one was going to bother her husband.

Yanal pleaded, and at last Paula let him into the house.

Ben-Gurion sat up in bed and blinked as Yanal excitedly told him the news.

"I don't believe it!" the Old Man said at first. But as he said it he was getting out of bed. "If it is true, I must broadcast to America."

He put his coat on over his pajamas, while Paula found his socks and shoes.

In the car on the way to the station he was quiet, thinking of what he wanted to say.

It was twenty minutes after five in the morning in Tel Aviv when Ben-Gurion began his first broadcast to the United States. But in New York it was twenty minutes after ten in the evening.

Five minutes later, while he was still on the air, the walls of the building suddenly trembled and the air was filled with a great noise. Ben-Gurion stopped talking for a moment and then calmly said into the microphone:

"The noise you just heard came from bombs dropped by enemy aircraft which are flying over our heads."

By the time the broadcast was finished, Yanal had learned by telephone that Egyptian planes had bombed Dov Airport, the secret Haganah landing field.

"I must go there and inspect the damage," Ben-Gurion declared.

They were just getting into Yanal's car when Ben-Gurion saw another car coming toward them. In it was Yadin.

"Are you going to the airport?" Ben-Gurion asked him.

"Yes," he answered.

"I'll go, too" Ben Gurion said.

"No," Yadin said. He insisted that his Commander-in-Chief should get some rest. The days ahead were going to be very hard. Then he drove off alone.

Half an hour after the first raid, more Egyptian planes came over Tel Aviv and headed for Dov Airport again. As they flew low, Yadin and the other Haganah men who were there threw themselves on the ground and held their breath.

After the planes had gone and Yadin was getting to his feet, he saw a man with a fringe of white hair coming toward him.

"Ben-Gurion!"

The Old Man grinned.

"How did you get here?" Yadin asked.

With a twinkle in his eye Ben-Gurion said that after Yanal had left him at his door he commanded one of the guards on duty in front of his house to drive him to the airport. He had arrived at just the right moment.

When Ben-Gurion finally went home again, Paula had his breakfast ready. As he was eating, Yadin came in. He looked very upset.

"The Egyptian Army has crossed the frontier and is bombarding our settlements," he said.

"We expected it," Ben-Gurion replied.

"The Arab Legion is moving, too. The Syrian Army as well," Yadin added.

"I had better go to headquarters with you," his chief decided.

Yadin nodded.

The Old Man went upstairs to change into battle dress.

Yadin waited.

Paula began washing the dishes.

CHAPTER FIFTEEN

From the moment the Egyptians bombed Dov Airport, Ben-Gurion thought of nothing but the war. Paula hardly ever saw him. Sometimes he came home to sleep for a few hours, but often he slept on a cot at general headquarters.

He was worried about Jerusalem. The United Nations said it was to be an international city. Ben-Gurion had always hoped that someday Jerusalem would belong to the Jews. Still, he had promised that Israel would obey all the decisions of the U.N. and he would keep his promise. But when the Arabs attacked Jerusalem and tried to make it theirs alone, and no one tried to stop them, he decided the Jews must defend Jerusalem and make it part of the State of Israel.

Now the city was cut off from Israel, for it was surrounded by Arabs. The problem was to clear a road to Jerusalem. But the Arab Legion was at Latrun, a town dominating the Tel Aviv-Jerusalem road. Ben-Gurion wanted the Army to meet the Arab Legion at Latrun. His officers did not think this was a good idea because of the weakness of the Jewish forces, but Ben-Gurion insisted, and he was the Commander-in-Chief.

So the 7th Armored Brigade was formed and the men were driven in buses to within five miles of Latrun, where they prepared to attack.

Ben-Gurion's officers were very upset by now. Yadin went to the front lines and sent the Commander-in-Chief a telegram:

"I beg you to order a delay of twenty-four hours."

The reply he received was very short: "No."

The 7th Armored Brigade attacked that night. Eight hundred men were killed or wounded, and the brigade had to retreat. The next night Ben-Gurion ordered them to try again. They failed a second time. Yadin finally brought in Yigal Allon, the best field commander in the Army, to lead a third attack. But it also failed.

But because of Ben-Gurion's persistence the Arab Legion had to take men and guns from Jerusalem to defend Latrun against the Israelis, so they were not able to force the Jews out of Jerusalem entirely.

After almost a month of war there was a truce. It was arranged by Count Folke Bernadotte of Sweden, who had been sent to the Middle East by the United Nations. Several weeks earlier Bernadotte and Ben-

Gurion had met for the first time at general headquarters. The tall blond count and the short, tough
Jewish Commander-in-Chief did not like each other
right away.

"I have come only to discuss a truce proposal,"
Bernadotte said. "I cannot deal with the whole problem of the future of Palestine."

There was something about the way he said it
that annoyed Ben-Gurion. On his part, Bernadotte
thought that Ben-Gurion was showing a "very bitter
spirit."

Ben-Gurion said to him:

"If there is a truce, Jews now separated from their
families in Jerusalem must be permitted to be re-
united with them."

When Bernadotte did not answer him, Ben-Gurion
went on:

"My own daughter Renana is in Jerusalem. I would
like to see her. I have not seen her for a long time."

Bernadotte replied quickly:

"Your official position as Commander-in-Chief will
place obstacles in the way of such a visit," subtly
reminding Ben-Gurion that Jerusalem was considered
by the U.N. as an international city.

They argued for a long time. Nothing was settled.
Finally the count looked at his watch and said he
must leave; he had promised to go to a concert with
a friend.

Nine days after the truce was signed, a ship called

the *Altalena* was seen coming toward the shores of Israel. She had been bought by American Jews to bring people and weapons to Israel. Many people knew about her, but most of them did not know that she belonged to the Irgun.

Count Bernadotte and his U.N. men knew about her. So did Ben-Gurion's young assistant, Israel Galili, for he had talked to the leader of the Irgun, Menachem Begin, about what to do with the weapons.

Before the mandate had ended, the Irgun had agreed to obey Haganah's rules and serve under Haganah's leaders. After Israel became a free country, one of Ben-Gurion's first orders was that all secret armies must disband. There was to be only one Army, Navy, and Air Force for Israel, and he was its Commander-in-Chief. The Irgun had defied this order.

So as the *Altalena* came close to Israel, Galili insisted that Begin turn over to the government the guns and ammunition she carried. Begin refused. He said that Irgun owned the ship, and the men on her were Irgun sailors, so he, and he alone, would hand out the guns.

Galili and Begin talked for many hours, and finally Begin said he would give the government some of the guns and send the rest to the Irgun fighters in Jerusalem. But Ben-Gurion ordered Galili to say no to this.

By now some of the weapons had been put ashore at Kfar Vitkin, a seaport about twenty-five miles north of Tel Aviv. Irgun men were deserting their posts on the front lines to help unload the *Altalena*, and the Israeli Army was waiting for orders from Ben-Gurion.

Bernadotte sent one of his U.N. men to see if it was true that guns were being put ashore, for both Israel and the Arabs had promised the U.N. that during the truce they would not bring any more weapons into their countries. But Bernadotte's man was not allowed to go near the place where the *Altalena* was being unloaded.

That evening, Ben-Gurion made a decision. This was the moment for Israel to show that it expected all of its people to obey its laws. He ordered the Army to disarm the Irgun forces at Kfar Vitkin and the Navy to take over the *Altalena*. They were to use their guns if necessary.

The unloading was stopped. The *Altalena* moved out to sea, and on each side of her was an Israeli ship. It looked as if Ben-Gurion had won, and not a shot had been fired.

But the next morning, after the Altalena had anchored at Tel Aviv, within sight of the hotel where Bernadotte's men were staying, Irgun men came ashore in a small boat, set up guns on the beach, and announced they would shoot Ben-Gurion, the Israeli Army, the U.N., and anyone else who tried to take their ship or its cargo.

Fighting began early that morning. First Irgun and Israeli army men and women began shooting at each other on shore.

Then Yigal Allon, chief of the Palmach commandos, was called to the general headquarters. Ben-Gurion himself ordered Allon to bring up an artillery piece and fire at the *Altalena.*

After Allon left, Ben-Gurion ordered all people except the soldiers and sailors to leave the place where the shooting was going on. His own house was not far away, so he telephoned Paula and told her of the danger. Then he said:

"Tell the neighbors to leave their houses until the trouble is over, and be sure that you go, too."

So Paula went from house to house, warning her neighbors. Then she came back to her own kitchen and went on with her housework. She wanted to wait there until her husband returned.

But she did not answer the telephone when it rang that afternoon. "I was afraid it might be Ben-Gurion, and I knew he would worry if he thought I was still here," she said.

Early in the afternoon Allon fired his artillery piece. One shell hit the guns and ammunition on the ship and set them on fire. There was a great explosion like Fourth of July fireworks, and the men and women on the ship jumped off and tried to swim for shore.

By nightfall, almost a hundred people were dead

or wounded. The *Altalena* was still burning, and there were crowds of excited people in the streets who wondered why this had to happen, just when there was a truce with the Arabs and things were getting better.

Begin went to the Irgun's secret radio station that evening and made a broadcast, screaming into the microphone until he had no voice left. The Irgun would not give up, he cried. The Irgun would defy the government. After that, Ben-Gurion ordered the police and the Army to round up all men and women who still belonged to the Irgun and put them in jail so they could not make any more trouble.

It saddened everyone to see Jews killing Jews, but after a little while many people realized that Ben-Gurion had been right. Israel would be a country where there was law and order, and where the government would get respect and obedience from all of the people.

In July the war with the Arabs began again, but by this time Israel had an Air Force. It was made up mostly of planes smuggled out of the United States, and its pilots were young Americans, Canadians, and Australians. Some of them were not even Jews.

The Israelis captured the Arab city of Ramle. Then Nazareth. Israeli planes bombed Cairo and Damascus. Israeli warships bombarded the city of Tyre, in Lebanon. Even the Arab Legion was driven back.

The Israelis won almost everywhere, but after ten

days of fighting Ben-Gurion agreed to another truce. He would try once more to make peace with the Arabs.

On September 17, 1948, while Ben-Gurion was at general headquarters in Tel Aviv, he received a telephone call from one of his men in Jerusalem.

"Count Bernadotte has been killed," he was told.

Bernadotte had been on his way to Jerusalem. His car had stopped when it came upon four men in a jeep that blocked the road. The men shot Bernadotte and the U.N. man who was sitting beside him. Then they escaped. The Stern Gang told everybody that their members had done the killing.

As soon as he heard this Ben-Gurion ordered the army commander in Jerusalem to arrest all members of the Stern Gang, find their secret hiding places, and take their guns away. He was also to close the roads leading out of Jerusalem so none of them could escape.

That evening, Ben-Gurion and his future Cabinet decided to give the Irgun until Tuesday to disband. They also said there would be a reward of twenty thousand dollars for whomever captured the killers of Count Bernadotte.

The leader of the Stern Gang, Nathan Friedman-Yellin, was caught at Haifa as he was about to leave the country. The Army rounded up hundreds of other members of the gang. Finally the Irgun obeyed Ben-Gurion's order and disbanded.

Bernadotte's killers were never caught, but another bad time for Israel had passed, and now not only his own people thought Ben-Gurion was a great man but people in many other countries of the world thought so, too.

Ben-Gurion spent most of his time at general headquarters. It was now October 1948 and the truce was still in force, but Israel itself was almost cut in two by the enemy. If war began again, Ben-Gurion wanted the Army to try once more to free all of Jerusalem.

"If we try and are defeated, the results may be terrible," said Yadin. Since Egypt was Israel's worst enemy, he told Ben-Gurion, if fighting were to break out again, he believed that they should try to defeat the Egyptians first.

Ben-Gurion called a meeting of his officers. Yigal Allon, now commander of the army in the south, asked to speak. He took a pointer and turned to a map.

"If we defeat the Egyptians in the Negev Desert we will then be able to come to Jerusalem from the rear," he said.

"We could skip Latrun.... We could cut around this way," he said as he moved his pointer on the map. "But first we must clear up the Negev."

Ben-Gurion listened, but he was not ready to tell Allon to go ahead with his plan. So Allon went back to his desert post and lent his small army plane to any settlers in the Negev who would go to general headquarters and beg Ben-Gurion to help them get rid of the Egyptian soldiers who were blocking their roads and cutting them off from the rest of their country.

Finally Ben-Gurion ordered the Army to go into the Negev Desert to begin Operation Ten Plagues, the name they had given to Allon's plan. Ten Plagues was very successful. In one week the Egyptians were running away everywhere except in the north of the Negev, at a place called Faluja. There a group of Egyptian soldiers kept fighting. One of them was a young captain named Gamal Abdel Nasser. Four years later he led a revolution and afterward became President of Egypt.

To get the Egyptians out of Faluja, the Israelis refused to let food be carried across the desert to Nasser and his men. The commanders of the Egyptian Army had a choice. They could let Captain Nasser and his men starve or they could attack the Israelis. They attacked, but they were defeated.

The Israelis were only a few miles outside the main headquarters of the Egyptians and were getting ready to start an attack that might have destroyed the Egyptian Army when a message came from general headquarters: "Stop all operations."

But Allon told his officers, "You prepare for an attack in the morning." Then he jumped into a jeep and drove to Beersheba. From there he flew in his private plane to Tel Aviv.

He wouldn't have been so puzzled by the order if he had known what had been going on in the rest of the world while he was planning to defeat the Egyptian Army.

It was Friday, December 31, the last day of the Christian year. That afternoon, Moshe Sharett, Israel's Minister of Foreign Affairs, had received a message from President Truman.

Great Britain had asked the United States to tell Israel that she would help the Egyptian Army unless the Israelis left Egyptian soil at once. President Truman also demanded that the Israelis leave Egypt and said that unless they left right away the United States might change its feeling about the Jewish state.

Meanwhile at headquarters Allon had found only an officer on duty. He asked where Yadin was. He had gone to bed, the officer said. Allon woke him up.

"We're losing a wonderful chance to destroy the whole Egyptian Army," Allon told him.

"President Truman has said it may change Israel-American friendship unless our troops leave," Yadin answered.

"I must see Ben-Gurion," Allon said.

"He's gone to Lake Tiberias," Yadin replied.

So Allon woke up Moshe Sharett instead. But Sharett also insisted they would have to get out of

Egypt. "We have made a promise to the American Government and we cannot possibly go back on our word," he told Allon.

"Then let me call the Old Man," Allon pleaded.

A telephone call was made to Ben-Gurion in Tiberias. He listened quietly to Allon's reasons for wanting to attack the Egyptians in the morning. Then he said: "Withdraw within twenty-four hours!" With that he put down the telephone and went back to sleep.

Soon afterward the Egyptians asked for a truce. The Israelis agreed, and the fighting stopped. Israel's War of Independence was over.

When Israel held her first election, to fill the 120 seats in the Knesset—or Parliament—Ben-Gurion's party, Mapai, won twice as many seats as any other party. The Knesset then elected Dr. Weizmann President of the State of Israel. The President would be a figurehead and would not govern the country, as the President in the United States does, but his position would be one of great honor. Everyone thought this honor should go to Dr. Weizmann. Then President Weizmann called on Ben-Gurion, the Prime Minister, to choose a Cabinet. Ben-Gurion did this happily, for now the last part of his dream was coming true. Israel was a free country with a real government, not just a Provisional Council, and with democratic institutions guaranteed by law.

CHAPTER SIXTEEN

Besides being Prime Minister, Ben-Gurion was Minister of Defense.

His day began at seven o'clock in the morning. By this time Paula was up and had breakfast ready for him. Then he would read the morning newspapers and after that work on government papers. He would walk to his office and be at his desk by nine o'clock. For the rest of the morning he talked to the chiefs of the Army, the Navy, and the Air Force.

At one-thirty he went home for lunch, and then he would work on government papers again. At four o'clock he went back to his office. There for the next four hours he would receive ambassadors from other countries, be interviewed by reporters, and have meetings with other members of the government.

He walked home at eight o'clock, always taking with him a briefcase full of papers. Sometimes he was accompanied by a member of the Cabinet with whom he wanted to talk.

Paula would have supper ready; usually it was cheese, bread, sour cream, and salad. They always ate in the kitchen, even when they had a guest.

For years there was a rule in the Ben-Gurion house, even after he became Prime Minister, that he and Paula would take turns washing the dishes. On the evenings when it was his turn he would hurry through his supper, even if a guest was there, wash his own dishes, and then stand waiting impatiently for the others to finish eating. If the guest insisted, he would be allowed to help clean up. Many famous and important Israelis washed dishes in the Ben-Gurion kitchen.

When supper was over and the guest had left, Ben-Gurion turned to his briefcase and worked on government papers again until midnight. The hours from midnight until two or three o'clock in the morning were always his favorite time of the day. Then he would prop himself up in a bed with a small light over his head and read for pleasure.

The Ben-Gurion house is in the north part of Tel Aviv. It is two stories high and made of stucco on the outside. Except for the wooden box of the guard in front of the door, it was just like hundreds of other houses around it.

On the first floor there were a living room, dining room, kitchen, Paula's room, and a small library. On the second floor were four rooms, three of them packed with books from the floor to the ceiling. Ben-

Gurion had his desk in the largest room, and also a globe of the world. In the second library there were a few chairs. Here he sometimes received old friends. The third library lead to his bedroom.

In the winter in Israel most people wear overcoats, the temperature often drops to the thirties, and people who live in modern houses turn on their central heating. But for years the only heat the Ben-Gurion's had came from an old-fashioned kerosene burner.

One day the American Ambassador, James G. McDonald, was invited for lunch and found Paula bundled up in heavy slacks and a sweater. That day the heater was first used to raise the temperature in the dining room a little above that of the inside of a refrigerator. Later the Prime Minister and Ambassador McDonald huddled over it in the living room, rubbing their hands together as they talked.

As Minister of Defense, Ben-Gurion had a military secretary, and as Prime Minister he had a director of the Prime Minister's office, an adviser on public relations, a private secretary, and two office assistants, as well as a stenographer and several typists.

From all these young people Ben-Gurion demanded hard work and loyalty, which they gave to him. But it was the military secretary who gave the most of himself. He was a young man named Nehemiah Argov, and he was a lieutenant colonel in the Army.

Argov was exactly as tall as the Prime Minister, five feet four inches. His dark hair was very different from his chief's white fringe. He had a sharp-pointed nose and unhappy eyes, and he seldom smiled. He was thin, but he was strong. While he was waiting somewhere for his chief he would often amuse himself by chinning on a door.

His loyalty to Ben-Gurion became known in every corner of Israel.

On nights when the Prime Minister stayed late at his desk, the staff would sit in the outer office, laughing, telling stories, sometimes talking about a movie they wanted to see if Ben-Gurion left soon enough. Argov would walk up and down nervously. After seeing that Ben-Gurion reached home safely he might join the others at a movie, but halfway through it he was likely to leave, saying:

"I'm sorry, but I'm worried about BG. I must see that everything is all right."

As military secretary he carried Ben-Gurion's orders to the Army and brought back to Ben-Gurion information his officers thought he should have. It was also his duty to make sure the Prime Minister was safe, just as the Secret Service does for the President of the United States. This was not easy during the war, when there were many Arabs in the country and constant danger of surprise air raids.

He passed on anyone who wanted to see the Prime Minister, and if he said no, that answer was final. At times he would walk a step or two behind Ben-Gurion, almost as if he were his shadow.

Argov had no selfish reason for doing all this and did not get a large salary. He only wanted to see that his commander was safe and happy.

Ben-Gurion called all his young associates by their first names, including Nehemiah. He insisted that they call him plain "Ben-Gurion." One of the typists was always making a mistake and saying, "Mr. Ben-Gurion." Each time she did, he would say, "Yes, *Miss* Mina!" emphasizing the MISS.

One day a young woman named Ruth Havilio was waiting in the outer office to be interviewed for a job as office assistant. As Ben-Gurion walked through the room, she jumped to her feet respectfully. The Prime Minister turned to her and said:

"Sit down!"

When she hesitated, he nodded toward Argov with a smile and said to her:

"He's a soldier and I am his commander, so I can order him to sit down. I suppose I must *ask* you."

Once, to welcome a new man to the office staff, Miss Havilio and Ben-Gurion's private secretary bought some flowers and put them on the new man's desk. With them there was a card that said:

With the Compliments of
The Prime Minister's
Personal Office

Then the staff signed their own first names on the card. Ben-Gurion passed through the office and saw the flowers. He picked up the card and read it.

"Where is my name?" he asked.

"You are the Prime Minister," Miss Havilio said.

"What do you mean, I am the Prime Minister? Were you never taught what colleagues are?" he demanded.

"I was also taught what a Prime Minister is," she answered.

"A Prime Minister is an office, not a man," Ben-Gurion told her seriously. "Someday there will be another Prime Minister. But I am a man!"

Then he took a pen and signed the card, "David," though hardly anyone called him that any more.

There was a great deal of work to be done in the office. Ben-Gurion's private secretary and two assistants saw all the letters that were received. The important ones were put on Ben-Gurion's desk and they answered the others themselves. In those first days of the new state, it seemed that most of the people of Israel had complaints, wanted something, or found another excuse to write to the Prime Minister, and they expected him to answer them. A man whose water pipes had burst ...a wife whose husband had run away ... people telling the Prime Minister how he should run the country.

It would have taken many Ben-Gurions to answer

them all, so the staff did it and signed the letters, "From the Prime Minister's Office." This would have worked out very well, except that the Prime Minister kept wandering into the outer office and taking letters from the pile on Miss Havilio's desk and walking off with them. Every letter interested him, and he would have liked to see them all.

One day a letter came from three Arabs. Now that there was a state they were writing to the Prime Minister to say that they would like jobs. Ben-Gurion saw the letter on Miss Havilio's desk, took it to his own office, and spent most of the afternoon telephoning people in the government, trying to find jobs for three out-of-work Arabs.

After that if anyone in the office had a letter he especially wanted Ben-Gurion to read, he would put it on the top of the mail at the corner of Miss Havilio's desk, and Ben-Gurion was almost sure to pick it up and walk off with it.

Ben-Gurion never dictated to a secretary, although he could speak seven languages. Instead he had a notebook and wrote his letters and orders in pencil. Then he tore out the sheets and walked to the outer office and handed them to a typist. No matter what language the letter was finally to be in, he always wrote in Hebrew. The office assistants translated the letters into English, or French, or whatever language was spoken in the country the letter was going to.

One day an English author came into the outer

office just as Miss Havilio finished translating a letter Ben-Gurion wanted to go out in English. She gave it to the author and asked him to make it a little better.

That evening Ben-Gurion came from his office, holding the letter in his hand.

"Whose letter is this?" he asked.

Miss Havilio confessed.

"It's very beautiful, but it's him, not me," Ben-Gurion said. "Now you translate it over again into my kind of English."

CHAPTER SEVENTEEN

Everything was peaceful for the moment in Israel, and Ben-Gurion could turn to the many tasks before him and try to prove to his own people and to the world that he could continue to be as great a leader as he had been during the war.

Israel was still a country without a capital city. Government offices were still at Hakirya, but the Knesset had no building of its own, so it had to meet in a movie theater in Tel Aviv.

Thousands of men and women were working in the new government offices, but it took time for them to learn their Jobs, and meanwhile people laughed at their mistakes and told stories, like the one about the two lions that escaped from the zoo. One lion stayed in Tel Aviv. The other decided it would be safer to go to the Negev Desert. A week later he came back to Tel Aviv, tired and hungry.

There hadn't been many people to eat in the desert. The Tel Aviv lion was plump and happy.

"Every morning at eight o'clock I go to Hakirya and stand outside the government and have a nice meal of five officials," he said.

"But isn't it dangerous?" asked the desert lion.

"Not at all," replied the Tel Aviv lion. "There are so many officials, nobody misses the few I take."

Ben-Gurion's working hours grew longer and longer. He made a four-year plan for Israel and had it printed so each government official could tack it on the wall over his desk. He said that each official should read it every morning and ask himself what he could do during the day to help make it come true.

The people wanted a Bill of Rights. Ben-Gurion replied impatiently:

"What we need right now is a Bill of Duties."

When there was talk about what a Bill of Rights should say, Ben-Gurion answered:

"It takes many words in English, but just three in Hebrew: *Veahavata lere-acha kamocha*." This means: Love your neighbor as yourself.

The gates of Israel were wide open now, and thousands of Jews were pouring in from all points of the compass—from France and Italy, Egypt and Ethiopia, China and India—from almost every country in the world. There were all kinds: white, yellow, and black; the sick, the well; tall, thin, short, some without an arm or a leg, laughing, crying; they spoke more than fifty different languages. Some, like the Yemenites, had come from primitive countries where even automobiles were almost unknown, but all were Jews. They had been away from their homeland for two thousand years, they were welcome now because every Jew in world had the right to come back.

Ben-Gurion was making greater plans for Israel than ever before, and he tried to tell his people how wonderful it was going to be one day. He said:

"We shall plant our trees in every unsown stretch of the countryside, and we shall remove the shame of desolation from all the soil of the homeland. The country will blossom and be beautiful again."

There were many hardships because so much work had to be done in so short a time. At first there was not nearly enough money to build all the houses that were needed. Food was scarce. Clothing was hard to get. But the Ben-Gurions lived like everyone else. Often Paula Ben-Gurion would stand in a line, like the rest of the housewives, and gossip with them while she waited her turn to buy.

Just as Ben-Gurion had set an example to the leaders of Israel in how to stay humble though he was an important man, so Paula had given the wives a few lessons. She talked with the guards outside her house about their families and gossiped with the neighbors. She had a woman come in to help her clean the house once in a while, but she never had a full-time maid. One of the few things she had bought for herself was an electric fan, which she kept on beside heir bed during the hot summer nights.

Soon after the war with the Arabs ended, a nephew in New York wrote her that he was coming to Israel and asked what she would like him to bring her from America. She could have chosen an electric toaster or blanket, or a beautiful dress or an air conditioner, but instead she said all she wanted were some packages of dried soup.

Ben-Gurion spent much of his time trying to encourage his people. When storms filled their tents with water and the food was bad, he gave them strength and hope—and he set about getting houses for them.

In the next few weeks twenty-five thousand houses would be finished. A billion trees would be planted on the hills. A police force of two thousand men had been created, and all were Jews. Never again in this country would anyone but another Jew arrest a Jew. There was an Israel airline. It had only one plane, but patience! The railroad was running again. Israel was alive. Israel was a nation.

In 1949 Israel became the fifty-ninth member of the United Nations. Three days after that Israel was one year old. There was much celebrating throughout the country.

In spite of all the work he had to do Ben-Gurion took off one day a month to visit the army camps and the farmers who lived near the frontiers. The Army became more important to him than ever before. It was a much better Army than it had been, and he saw now that it could not only defend Israel against her enemies but also unite and educate the people.

Jews from the Arab countries and from Europe were taken by the Army and made into Israelis. At eighteen, young Israelis are required to undergo compulsory military training, girls for two years, boys for two and a half years. Girls who marry before the conscription age are excepted. The Army taught them all to speak Hebrew. It taught those from remote parts of the world to use knives and forks, to sleep in beds instead of on the floor, to brush their teeth. It taught them Jewish history, geography, how to use soap, and how to read. Best of all, it taught them to live together as brothers.

Toward the end of the year Ben-Gurion was forced to decide what he was going to do about Jerusalem. After so many months of fighting, the New City was a sad place. There had been people killed in almost every street, and almost every family had lost a loved one.

While the United Nations talked about the future of Jerusalem, Ben-Gurion and his Cabinet tried to rebuild the part of the city they governed. They began to erect new houses. Ten thousand immigrants were sent there. Businessmen were encouraged to move there.

Then they learned that the United Nations had decided to send a council to rule Jerusalem. It was not to be a Jewish city.

Ben-Gurion did not hesitate. In spite of the United Nations, he declared that the modern part of Jerusalem called the New City, which was held by the Jews, would be the capital of Israel.

Some Israelis were upset because he had defied the U.N. After all, they said, the U.N. had created Israel. But others answered that almost all the people in the New City were Jewish and that the people of Israel could not just forget about them. Besides, this was the ancient city of David. For thousands of years Jews had been praying to return there.

During the autumn, Ben-Gurion had quietly moved several government departments to Jerusalem. Then he climbed into his car and drove the forty-five miles from Tel Aviv to Jerusalem. He announced that from then on the Knesset would meet in Jerusalem. All government departments would be there except Defense and Foreign Affairs. They would stay in Tel Aviv.

Nearly two years earlier, Ben-Gurion had left Jerusalem to become Commander-in-Chief of the Army, Navy, and Air Force. As he left his office in the Jewish Agency building, he had slipped the key into his pocket and said: "I think I'll keep this. I am sure I will be coming back."

Now the time had come to use the key again.

CHAPTER EIGHTEEN

At the start of 1950 the Prime Minister and his staff moved into the old Jewish Agency building.

Ben-Gurion's private office was a room on the second floor, with maps on the walls. The one behind his desk was very large and showed the Arab countries in red, the rest of the world in yellow, and Israel as a blue dot, so small it could hardly be seen.

"It reminds me every day how small we are," Ben-Gurion said.

On the desk was a calendar showing the date, both by Jewish and Christian months, a black iron machine for punching holes in paper, a marble stand holding two fountain pens, a Bible, and four telephones.

There were six leather chairs surrounding the desk. An oriental rug covered part of the floor. At the far end of the room there was a coffee table, two comfortable chairs, and a sofa. There were also several shelves of books. It was only a few steps from the

Prime Minister's office to the Cabinet's room, where sixteen brown leather chairs surrounded a huge table.

At first the Ben-Gurions lived in a hotel in Jerusalem, but later the government bought a house for them to use on Ben Maimon Avenue, almost across the street from the house of Yigael Yadin and his wife.

So Paula found herself with two homes to take care of. Still, she would not have a full-time maid in either house.

The house on Ben Maimon Avenue, like the one in Tel Aviv, was two stories high, and it had a large garden. On the second floor Ben-Gurion had a small library, but he still kept most of his books in Tel Aviv, because it remained home to him.

In October he and Paula went away for the first vacation they had had in a long time. They went to Greece by airplane.

Ben-Gurion visited Athens and climbed the Acropolis. He visited an ancient outdoor theater and many other places he knew so well from his reading. He tried to talk to the Greeks in the classical language of their ancestors, but neither taxi drivers nor hotelkeepers, nor even professors, understood him. Finally he told the Greeks they should do what the Jews had done: learn the language of their ancestors and speak it everywhere in their country, as the Jews spoke Hebrew in Israel.

Just before midnight one evening in December an

extraordinary event took place. Eliahu Elath, a member of the Israel Government, was at London Airport in England to meet some people who were coming from Tel Aviv. As the passengers left the plane, he was surprised to see the white hair of the Prime Minister.

Ben-Gurion smiled when he saw Elath. He was traveling secretly, he explained. But the secret was not kept for very long. The London newspapers printed many stories about the visit of the Prime Minister and tried to guess why he was there. What had happened in Israel to bring the Prime Minister to England? they asked. Whom was he going to see? Where was he staying? Why was he hiding?

A reporter for a magazine solved the mystery.

There was nothing wrong. Ben-Gurion was not in hiding. He was in Oxford, and he had come all this way to spend a few days browsing among the stacks of one of the most famous bookshops in the world, Blackwell's.

Many people didn't believe the story. This was not the way any Prime Minister had ever acted before.

But the reporter wrote:

"In this age of barbarism, it is a pleasant thought that anyone who penetrated to the back rooms of Blackwell's last week and spied a little white-haired man on the top of a stepladder would have seen a Prime Minister indulging his secret vice."

CHAPTER NINETEEN

Nineteen fifty-one was an unforgettable year in the life of Ben-Gurion, and it started off in a very unusual way. One of the first things he did was to go to a camp near the seaside where the new immigrants lived. There he was *sandek*, or godfather, to a baby boy named David Yitzhak. Baby David's father and mother had just come from Iraq, and they had decided before they ever got to Israel to name their baby, if it was a boy, after the Prime Minister. Baby David was their fourteenth child, and he cried long and loud all through the ceremony.

So many pictures of the event were printed in the newspapers that it caused hundreds of other mothers and fathers to name their boys after the Prime Minister, until he had his secretary announce that he could not be *sandek* for any more babies.

In February there was trouble in the Knesset. The Orthodox members wanted the right to decide what the immigrant children would be taught about their religion. Ben-Gurion said no; only the State of Israel should have this right, he declared. But most of the Knesset disagreed with him, so he resigned as Prime Minister and asked that the people elect a new Knesset. President Weizmann asked him to stay on as temporary Prime Minister until elections could be held in the summer, and he agreed. Then, with Paula and Argov and several newspapermen, he went to the United States.

Ben-Gurion had visited the United States before, but at those times hardly anyone noticed when he arrived. This time he came as a famous man. He flew in a big blue and white airplane-on the first trip across the Atlantic Ocean of Israel's own airline, El Al. The plane landed first at Washington, and there Ben-Gurion paid his respects to President Truman. Then he and his party went on to New York.

No Jew had ever received such a wonderful welcome as Ben-Gurion got in New York. There was a parade led by thirty-six motorcycles, then twenty cars full of important people. They were followed by thousands of American soldiers, sailors, and airmen marching to the music of a band. Then came sailors from Israel, and hundreds of policemen and firemen.

As Ben-Gurion rode along Broadway in a car with the top down, he was showered with bits of paper and torn-up telephone books. The police chief said that a million and a half people came to see him. "Why, that's more than all the people in Israel!" one of Ben-Gurion's companions exclaimed that night when he read the figure in the paper.

At City Hall, where he and Paula had been married, there were a hundred thousand people marching as the mayor welcomed Ben-Gurion. Then the mayor proclaimed it Ben-Gurion Day.

While they were in New York, Ben-Gurion, Paula, and Argov stayed in an apartment at the Waldorf-Astoria Hotel. Another guest who was staying there at the same time was General Douglas MacArthur, the famous commander of World War II.

On his second night in New York, Ben-Gurion began the Bonds for Israel drive at Madison Square Garden. The money raised would go to build houses and roads, ships and harbors, and the other things a new country needed. The Garden was packed with people eager to hear him speak, and outside, crowds stood in the streets to hear him on the loudspeakers that had been put up.

Israel's brilliant young Ambassador to the United States, Abba Eban, introduced Ben-Gurion to the audience.

By the time the Prime Minister rose to speak, they were cheering wildly. That night they promised to buy thirty-five million dollars' worth of bonds for Israel.

On his fourth day—trailed by a police captain and two detectives in plain clothes—he went browsing in several bookshops. Altogether he bought almost thirty books.

During his visit to the United States, Prime Minister David Ben-Gurion presented President Harry S. Truman with a menorah on behalf of the citizens of the State of Israel. Looking on is the young Israeli Ambassador to the United States, Abba Eban.

(Israel State Archives)

No matter where Ben-Gurion went he was always in need of hearing the latest news from around the world. Here on military maneuvers, he tries to tune in *Kol Yisroel* on his new portable radio. *(Israel State Archives)*

His leadership was an inspiration to the people of Israel and especially to its soldiers who saw in him a wise, prudent leader. The expression on the face of Chief of Staff Yigal Yadin expresses the affection and respect which Israel's top general in 1949 felt for his Prime Minister. *(Israel State Archives)*

Ben-Gurion's closest aide was a young and gifted military assistant Nehemiah Argov. Here they are seen sailing together aboard a vessel of the Israeli Navy. *(Israel State Archives)*

Ben-Gurion also enjoyed exploring the territory of the State of Israel on the ground. Despite his advancing years he had a nimble stride which is seen here during a visit to Avdat Springs. *(Israel State Archives)*

At a press conference in the Netherlands in June of 1960, Ben-Gurion was colorful in making his audience understand the key points of his talk. "You understand,"

"Things may get better . . ."

"Or they may get worse."

"But I'm sure everything is for the best."
(Israel State Archives)

Ben-Gurion arrives in Sde Boker
(© *Werner Braun*)

By 1954, Ben-Gurion had begun to live and work on a kibbutz in the Negev, Sde Boker, which was to be his home for the rest of his life. Here in his study in December 1954, he is at work on his memoirs. *(Israel State Archives)*

At Sde Boker, Ben-Gurion learned to take care of sheep. He was attentive to their teeth but Mrs. Ben-Gurion was more worried that he might lose a finger or two. *(Israel State Archives)*

Ben-Gurion lived simply. This is his bedroom at Sde Boker.
(Israel State Archives)

This is Ben-Gurion's home at Sde Boker, the famous Green Hut. Rooms were added on until it became large enough for him and Mrs. Ben-Gurion to live comfortably.
(Israel State Archives)

On Sunday the Prime Minister went by car to Princeton, New Jersey, to visit the best-known Jew in the world, the famous physicist, Professor Albert Einstein. The day was mild, and they sat outdoors in the garden chairs, side by side.

They posed for newspaper pictures, smiling at each other and shaking hands. They looked a bit alike. Both of them had a great deal of white hair that almost covered their ears, and they smiled in the same way, with two broad smiles that showed great delight.

After the reporters left, they sat alone and talked. For years Ben-Gurion had admired Einstein, and later when he was telling one of his friends about the visit he said:

"Do you realize that Einstein is a scientist who needs no laboratory, no equipment, no tools of any kind? He just sits in an empty room with a pencil and a piece of paper, and his brain, thinking."

From New York, Ben-Gurion went on a tour of the whole country.

In Philadelphia he saw the Liberty Bell, and in Baltimore he was given the keys to the city. In Washington he was the guest of honor at a huge and beautiful party. He also went to Boston, Detroit, Cleveland, and Chicago, and finally Los Angeles. There was a big meeting in the Hollywood Bowl, and the celebrated movie actor Edward G. Robinson read Israel's Declaration of Independence. One of

Hollywood's greatest movie producers, and a founder of MGM, Samuel Goldwyn introduced Ben-Gurion to the audience, and they laughed when Ben-Gurion told them with a smile that the weather in California was almost as good as the weather in Israel.

Ben-Gurion and Paula and their party had stayed in the United States about a month when it was time for them to leave. But during this short visit they had helped sell fifty-five million dollars' worth of bonds for Israel.

Once more they stepped aboard the big blue and white plane they had come in and flew back home. As the plane came near the shores of their homeland, six Israeli airplanes came up to meet it. On the ground there was an honor guard of airmen, sailors, girl soldiers, the entire Cabinet and general staff, many members of the Knesset, the United States Ambassador to Israel, and thousands of ordinary people. They had all come to welcome home David Ben-Gurion, the great leader of Israel.

Ben-Gurion came back from America full of energy, and it was good that he did, because he was going to be very busy getting ready for the elections that were to take place in the summer.

His Mapai party had run the government for more than three years, and now it was being blamed for everything that anyone thought was wrong with the country: not enough food, not enough money. Some people said his government was too eager to fight with the Arabs, and others said it was too nice to them. But Ben-Gurion always had faith in the people, so he went straight to them. They crowded into his meetings. He told them they would have to work hard to make Israel strong, so that she would be safe from her enemies. They would have to work hard to grow more food, so there would be enough for everybody and no one would go hungry. He promised to guide them, but he would not make any promises he could not keep.

"I will not promise to find a husband and a new dress for every woman, or a wife and a new suit for every man in Israel," he told them with a twinkle in his eye, and they laughed.

The election was held in August. Hundreds of thousands of new people in Israel voted for the first time. When all the votes were counted, Ben-Gurion's party had won more seats in the Knesset than any other party. He was again Prime Minister.

CHAPTER TWENTY

In February 1952 Ben-Gurion met a man he had known more than thirty years earlier. The man's name was Sam Hamburg. He and Ben-Gurion had been in the Jewish Legion together in World War I. After the war he left Palestine and went to America. There he borrowed money to study farming in California. By 1952 he had become very rich, for he had learned how to grow fruits and vegetables in the desert of California, and he had a ranch almost as big as Manhattan!

Ben-Gurion knew all about him: his wheat crop had been destroyed by rust, his wells had dried up, but he overcame his troubles with hard work and courage. Once he had even made a river run forty miles uphill! It was Jews like this that Israel needed, the Prime Minister thought. So he sent for Sam Hamburg.

Hamburg visited the *kibbutzim*—the collective

farms—and then went to tell Ben-Gurion about what
he had seen.

"Your farming here is no good," he said to the
Prime Minister bluntly.

"Why not?" Ben-Gurion asked.

"Your people plant tiny fields with tiny plants,
the way they used to do in Europe," Hamburg replied.

"What should we do?" Ben-Gurion wanted to
know.

"Mr. Prime Minister, this is the best soil in the
world. You have a uniform climate. You could grow
fine cotton here, and sugar, tobacco, peanuts, grains,
winter vegetables."

Ben-Gurion raised his bushy eyebrows.

"You could export. Do a big business," Hamburg
went on.

"Our scientists tell me we can't raise cotton because of a bad insect," Ben-Gurion said.

Hamburg waved the idea aside with one of his
big hands.

"There is no insect in the world that can't be
controlled, and economically, too, if you raise large
enough crops," he answered.

They talked for a long time. Finally the Prime
Minister hit his desk with his hand and said:

"How about coming to the Negev with me next
week?"

"Impossible," Hamburg answered. "It's spring back in California already. I have crops to put in. But I'll tell you what I'll do. I'll return later if you want me to."

"When?" asked Ben-Gurion.

Hamburg pulled a small diary out of his pocket and looked at it.

"I'll meet you in front of your office on March 6—that's a Thursday—at eight o'clock in the morning," he said.

Ben-Gurion grinned. This was the sort of man he liked.

"You'll surely be here?" he said.

"Certainly!" Hamburg answered.

On Thursday, March 6, at a quarter to eight in the morning Ben-Gurion and about fifty other men were in front of the Ministry of Defense in Tel Aviv. Several cars stood at the curb. Chief of Staff Yadin was there, and there were also some members of the Cabinet, and many scientists.

They kept looking at their watches, for some of them had bet that Sam Hamburg would not come.

At exactly eight o'clock he arrived, and they all started for the Negev. They toured the desert the whole day and saw thousands of acres of land that looked as if it never could grow anything.

Finally they stopped at a village, and Ben-Gurion asked:

"Well, Hamburg, what do you think?"

"That last place we visited," he answered. "I can tell you that when you get water there you can produce some of the finest cotton and sugar in the world."

This advice from Sam Hamburg was the start of cotton growing in the Negev Desert.

Before he left Israel that time, Hamburg asked Ben-Gurion for a piece of land that all the scientists said was worthless. On this land he said he would build a model farm.

Ben-Gurion gave him some land two hundred feet above the Jordan River—yellow, dry land covered with weeds and wild pigs.

"How are you going to get water up here?" the Israelis asked him.

"God and me—we'll do it together," he answered.

Late in the year the Prime Minister and Yadin had a serious disagreement. Yadin had been made chief of staff with orders to reorganize the Army. The disagreement came over money. Ben-Gurion had decided that there was not going to be a war with the Arabs for a while and therefore the Army's budget could be cut. Instead the money could be spent on new schools, roads, and houses that the people needed.

This disturbed Yadin. "I know your economic problems," he told Ben-Gurion, "but you must let me have the same budget for one more year; otherwise you will have to find another commander."

Ben-Gurion was sorry to see Yadin leave, but it did not change his mind.

About this time Dr. Chaim Weizmann died. The people of Israel and Jews all over the world were sad when they heard the news, and Ben-Gurion bowed his head as he walked in the funeral procession.

Then the Knesset had to choose someone to take his place as President. Ben-Gurion suggested that they ask Einstein.

"I am almost certain he will not accept, but it would be wrong not to offer the position to the greatest living Jew," he said.

Einstein did not want to be President, and so Ben-Gurion suggested Itzhak Ben-Zvi, a life long leader of the *Yishuv* who had been his friend for many years. After several votes were taken, Ben-Zvi was elected President of Israel.

CHAPTER TWENTY-ONE

In June of 1954 Sam Hamburg was back in Israel. He had planted cotton on ten acres of his model farm and now he had come to look at the crop. One day he arrived at the Prime Minister's office with a whole plant in his hand. He greeted Ben-Gurion by holding it out before him and saying:

"Look!...Look at that plant! I have never seen such luxuriant cotton in June, and I've been raising it for thirty years."

Ben-Gurion took the plant, felt the cotton with his fingers, then smiled.

"Israel thanks you" he said.

Hamburg fumbled with his hat.

"No, Mr. Prime Minister, I must thank you. I never thought cotton could be so... important. I never imagined that a little ten-acre field could give me a greater feeling of purpose... than anything else on earth."

On a summer day when the Negev Desert seemed like the inside of a boiling kettle and the sand was burning hot, Ben-Gurion made a trip to the port of Eilat with a group of soldiers. On the way they stopped at a place called Avdat. There they met some young men who said they were from a *kibbutz* nearby. Their *kibbutz* was named Sde Boker, which means Field of the Cattleman, and they were looking for a place that would be good for raising sheep.

Sde Boker was only a little way from the main road, so Ben-Gurion and his party stopped there on their way home.

The *kibbutz* was just a year old, and there were not many people living on it yet. So far it had only a few wooden buildings.

Living on the *kibbutz* was hard, and sometimes dangerous.

When strong winds blew across the desert, it was impossible to see your hand before your face. The wind was so hot that it seemed to blister your face, and it would often lift the sand and mix it with the air, and then drive it into your eyes and ears, and into the tiniest cracks in the houses. There was danger from unfriendly Arabs and from poisonous snakes. The Sde Boker settlers caught two or three cobras every month.

For seven months of every year there was no rain, and the sun baked the earth until it was as hard and dry as steel. During the other months there would be heavy rainstorms, and the water would run down the dry desert hills and collect in big puddles. As Jews had done in ancient times, these young settlers built dams of earth to make small lakes. From here they would carry the water to their fields as it was needed.

Water for people and for animals had to be brought in by trucks.

When Ben-Gurion got back to his office in Jerusalem he gathered his staff around him and told them of all he had seen at Sde Boker.

"I am jealous of those young people," he said. "What a wonderful experience!"

From time to time in the days that followed he said:

"No one is indispensable."

That was something he had often said. But now he added:

"Older people should give younger people a chance."

Finally he asked Paula:

"How would you like to live in the desert?"

Paula decided she would go wherever her husband wished. She knew that life is not easy in any *kibbutz*, and they were no longer young. In the desert it might be more than they could bear. But she knew Ben-Gurion wanted to go, and she wanted her husband to be happy.

Ben-Gurion announced that he had decided to resign as Prime Minister and Minister of Defense and move to Sde Boker. But he would still be a member of the Knesset.

When his followers in the Knesset first heard the news, they were so surprised they could not speak.

Then, one by one, they asked him to change his mind. But Ben-Gurion sat in his chair, silent. He had made his decision and he refused to change it.

Paula was kept busy answering the phone and telling people she was sorry but she could not let them speak to Ben-Gurion. Letters and telegrams asking him to stay piled up.

Everybody was talking about the Prime Minister's leaving and trying to guess why he was going. Some people thought he wanted time to read and write books. Others felt he was disappointed in the young people of Israel. He thought they were more interested in chewing gum, lipstick, and the movies than they were in going to the *kibbutzim* to grow trees and build houses to make Israel a country of people who were strong and happy.

He was disappointed that so many of the immigrants insisted on settling in Tel Aviv. Here they crowded the restaurants and tried to open small shops. They refused to go on to the land and become farmers, even though Israel needed farmers.

Because of this, many people thought Ben-Gurion was going to the Negev to set an example for his people, since he had not been able to persuade them with his words.

On Monday morning, December 7, 1954, Ben-Gurion sent his resignation to President Ben-Zvi. It said:

"No one man is indispensable to a state, and certainly I am not.... Israel is not leaderless.... My friend Moshe Sharett will be Acting Prime Minister.... I am confident that a new government will be formed and approved by the Knesset without any undue delay or upheavals."

In the evening he made a farewell speech on the radio to the nation.

The following Sunday, Paula and Ben-Gurion rose earlier than usual. There was still some last minute packing to do. Before they even finished breakfast, callers began to arrive—government officials and old friends who wanted to say goodbye.

Their household goods were put in a truck. Jeeps filled with soldiers were waiting to escort the Ben-Gurions to their new home.

As they were leaving the house for the last time, Ben-Gurion turned to Paula and said:

"Did you pack that cotton plant Sam Hamburg gave me?"

Paula assured him she had.

Then the retired Prime Minister shook hands with the policemen who had stood guard outside his house for so many years.

As they entered the car, Ben-Gurion looked at the crowd that had gathered. Some of the people were wiping their eyes with handkerchiefs. He waved his hand toward them and said:

"Do not weep. Follow me."

CHAPTER TWENTY-TWO

A swirl of brown dust billowing up into the air from a line of cars announced to the settlers of Sde Boker that the Ben-Gurions had arrived. Paula was the first to step to the ground. Her arms were full of flowers that had been given to her when they stopped at a village on the way.

As the secretary of the *kibbutz* came up to say, "Welcome," Paula thrust the flowers into his hands.

"If there's anyone sick, give them these," she said. "But they'd better be put in water right away."

Everyone helped unload the truck with the Ben-Gurions' furniture and books. Then the former Prime Minister ordered his military policemen to tell the newspaper photographers that each of them could take one picture and then they must go. It was not fair to these hard-working settlers to upset their routine and make a Roman holiday, he said.

The reporters wanted to ask a few questions.

"What will your job be here?" they asked Ben-Gurion.

"I have no idea," he answered. "This is a *kibbutz*. There is a secretary to arrange such matters.... I shall do what he gives me to do."

He waved aside their other questions, saying:

"When I have been here a few years I will be able to make a statement about what is happening and the chances of the future."

By late afternoon, reporters, photographers, friends, and the military police had all left, and the Ben-Gurions were in their new home.

"Welcome to Sde Boker," Ben-Gurion said to his wife, smiling.

"I hope you will be happy here," she answered warmly.

Then she started to set the house in order, while he began to arrange his books.

Their first visitor was a boy named Chemi Cohen, who was only four and a half years old. The front door was open, and Chemi wandered into the house. When he saw the white-haired man putting books on a shelf he stopped.

"Who are you?" he asked.

The former Prime Minister smiled at him and answered:

"I am the newest pioneer."

When Paula first saw the house they were to live in she said to her husband:

"This reminds me of the bungalow at Coney Island some girl friends and I rented one summer when I lived in New York."

The house was the color of mustard and had only three rooms. There was a screened porch across the front of the house, and it faced Sde Boker's office building, its air-raid shelter, and its community house.

Everyone at Sde Boker got up at a quarter to six in the morning and worked until four o'clock in the afternoon. Evenings were spent mostly in reading and making plans for the *kibbutz*.

Everyone ate in the community dining room. Breakfast was from eight to eight-thirty, lunch from twelve thirty to one, supper at seven o'clock in the evening. Some of the men wore khaki shorts, some wore long trousers. But only a few of them wore shirts. The girls dressed in shorts or slacks and a blouse. The only people who wore shoes were the ones who had just come to the *kibbutz*, because their feet weren't used to the heat of the sand.

Sde Boker had almost thirty acres planted with peach trees, grapes, and vegetables, but most of its land was left for the animals to graze. There were hundreds of sheep, two cows, a dozen horses, and thousands of chickens. The settlers sheared the sheep, carded the wool, dyed it, and used it to make rugs.

They could water their fields only between midnight and dawn. The rest of the time the winds were so strong they blew the water away.

At least one of the settlers was always on guard, day and night, and he was armed with a machine gun, for the people of Sde Boker feared that Arabs might attack them. Two settlers already had been killed mysteriously.

Once a month a truck went to Tel Aviv for supplies. There was electricity for six hours each day, but water was very scarce and each family was allowed to use only a certain amount. But the settlers had radios and they could get programs from Cairo and Tel Aviv.

Ben-Gurion's first job was to work in the fields. Later he became a shepherd. Paula was assigned to work in the community kitchen and the nursery.

After they had been there a few weeks a new settler arrived, a girl named Ruth Gil'adi. She was a *sabra*, with dark hair and sparkling eyes. She and Ben-Gurion often worked together, and they became friends. She was his idea of what Israel's youth should be like. She was pretty, intelligent, and brave.

She never spoke to him unless he began the conversation. Sometimes he would say nothing for a long time while they worked and he seemed to be thinking of things far away. But then suddenly he would turn to her and ask:

"What is the trouble with the young people of Israel? Why aren't there thousands like you in the Negev?"

She answered:

"We had our glorious hours during the war, didn't we? After that ... maybe we got lazy. Maybe we wanted a soft life."

In May the sheep-rearing season began. By this time Ben-Gurion felt wonderful. He would lift lambs that weighed more than a hundred pounds and put them on the table, and then he and Ruth would clip the wool. During these weeks Ruth looked very happy, because, she confided to her new friend, she had a wonderful secret. She was going to be married in June to a tall and handsome young settler named Zeev Steinhardt.

The arrival of the Ben-Gurions caused some problems for the *kibbutz*. Tourists, government people, diplomats from foreign countries, reporters, and photographers came to Sde Boker, sometimes many of them in a single day. They had to be fed, and sometimes rooms had to be found for them to sleep in overnight.

Toward the end of February a group of reporters came to see Ben-Gurion. They found him tan from working in the sun, and happy. There were too many of them for the small house, so Ben-Gurion invited them to sit around on the ground outside.

"It's good earth, and no dishonor to sit on it," he told them.

They asked him how well he thought the new government was running Israel. But he only said:

"I am not a member of the government any more. I am just a member of the Knesset who is working in a stable."

They asked what his work was, and he replied:

"At the moment, I'm looking after the kids and the goats in the barn."

When the reporters asked him about his plans for the future, he refused to talk about them, but of the Negev's future he said:

"One day this area may develop into the main center of population of Israel. The only problem is water."

Then he glanced affectionately toward the settlers who were standing around and added:

"The people here in the Negev are a little crazy, but I happen to like crazy people."

In June, Sam Hamburg arrived with an unusual gift: a small bale of cotton, the first ever ginned in Israel. As he placed it on the table in front of Ben-Gurion, Paula came into the room and asked:

"What on earth is that?"

"This, Paula, is the most important thing in Israel right now," her husband answered.

Ben-Gurion had a faraway look in his eyes as he stared at the cotton. After all, it had been grown on soil that the experts said was worthless. Sam Hamburg guessed what he was thinking.

Respect for work. Pride in work well done. Understanding the importance of a field of cotton, an orange grove, a sugar field. This was what Ben-Gurion wanted to teach his people.

Then Hamburg went with him to the barn and watched the white-haired ex-Prime Minister feeding barley to the lambs. Later he said:

"Looking at him ... I thought of Biblical prophets in that sheep barn at Sde Boker that night. . . ."

During that year Ben-Gurion made everyone in Israel aware of the desert, of what a wonderful place it could become, and how important it would be to Israel in the future.

One day in Tel Aviv, a simple shoemaker stopped Baruch Tal, one of Ben-Gurion's friends in the Knesset, as he was passing by and asked:

"Can you get me the measurements of the Old Man's feet?"

Tal asked why he wanted them, and he said:

"Well, I've been thinking a lot about him down there in the desert. They tell me it gets cold at night this time of year. I think of him down there, suffering, maybe. He's not a young man. He's older than I am. So he's down there suffering in the desert and here I am, just an ordinary man, living in comfort in Tel Aviv. So I think I'd like to make him a pair of shoes. It would help my conscience to feel better."

CHAPTER TWENTY-THREE

One day early in 1955, Minister of Labor Golda Myerson (who later took the Hebrew name of Meir) traveled to Sde Boker. She came to tell Ben-Gurion about the troubles his old followers were having keeping the Cabinet together. She also brought an invitation from Prime Minister Sharett for Ben-Gurion to return to the government as Minister of Defense. He could help prevent any more trouble until elections were held in the summer.

Three days later Sharett told the people that Ben-Gurion had agreed to come back. Then a few days afterward Ben-Gurion arrived in Jerusalem in his army uniform and was sworn in as Minister of Defense.

But he did not entirely leave Sde Boker. He arranged to keep the mustard-colored house. He left his books there, and he and Paula promised that they would return often. When he left he gave the *kibbutz* a present of two camels, for herding sheep.

In July, candidates began to campaign for election to the Knesset. Ben-Gurion made many speeches, and when the elections were over he was once again the leader of Israel.

In September, Prime Minister Nasser of Egypt announced that his country had agreed to buy weapons from Czechoslovakia. The members of the Israeli Government were once more worried that Egypt and the Arab countries might attack Israel.

Her safety once again became Israel's most important problem, and the Minister of Defense was the most important member of the Cabinet. His job was to get weapons for Israel, but it was very discouraging, for most countries did not want to sell her weapons. They were afraid that if they did, it might help start a new war between the Arabs and the Jews.

On a chilly day in November, Ben-Gurion made his first speech to the Knesset as the new Prime Minister and it was a bold speech. He said:

"It is my duty to tell all the powers that rule the world ... that the people of Israel will not be led like cattle to the slaughter.

On Ben-Gurion's orders that night a thousand Israel soldiers went off in trucks on a secret military adventure.

Forty miles southwest of Beersheba, on the Negev-Sinai border, there was a peace zone set up by the United Nations, near a place called El' Auja. For weeks the U.N. commissioner had been ordering the Egyptians to stop bringing soldiers and guns into the zone, but they continued to do it.

That night, the Israelis blackened their faces so they couldn't be seen in the bright moonlight. Then they attacked the Egyptians inside the zone. They fought for many hours, and finally the Egyptians moved back, into their own country. Five Israelis had been killed and several of them were hurt, but they took nearly fifty Egyptian prisoners.

In December there was more fighting, this time with the Syrians. Lake Tiberias had been given to Israel by the United Nations, but for years the Syrians had been shooting at Israeli fishermen who went out on the lake. Many of them had been killed. So in December the Israelis attacked the Syrians in return. They came back with twenty-nine Syrian prisoners, two pieces of Syrian artillery, and six of their own men dead. They left behind fifty-five dead Syrians.

The attack had been Ben-Gurion's idea, and he took full responsibility for it.

Nothing Israel had ever done had caused so much excitement and argument among the countries of the world. In the United Nations meetings some countries said Israel should be punished and others even said she should be expelled from the U.N.

Foreign Minister Sharett was very disturbed because he thought it was important for the world to have a good opinion of Israel. But Ben-Gurion faced the people who criticized him—both in Israel and outside of it—without backing down.

If no one was going to protect Israel, if there was no lawful way of punishing those who killed Israeli fishermen, then the state must do what she had done. Otherwise, before long the countries around her would be bold enough to march into Israel from all sides again, as they had done in 1948.

CHAPTER TWENTY-FOUR

Early in 1956 most of the world knew there was going to be more trouble between Israel and her Arab neighbors. Fights between Israel and Arab soldiers on the borders were taking place more often. The Arabs sent commandos into Israel at night to bomb houses and blow up roads and trucks. Many people had been killed.

Now Ben-Gurion, who had been criticized by some of his own people for ordering the attack on the Syrians, was being criticized by them for not declaring war on the Arabs. But he answered them by saying:

"We believe keeping the peace is better even than victory in war. War is right only in absolute self-defense."

In March each Israel soldier, sailor, and airman gave one day of work to the settlements near the borders so they would be strong enough to defend themselves if the Arabs attacked. They built walls, strung up barbed wire, and brought guns and ammunition. To set an example to his people Ben-Gurion drove with Nehemiah Argov, his military aide, from Jerusalem to a village near the Gaza border and helped string up barbed wire. There was a cold morning wind blowing from the desert, and Argov handed him a pair of gloves, but he threw them to the ground.

"A man is given hands to work with," he said

In June there was good news for Ben-Gurion: France had agreed to sell arms to Israel secretly. In the next four months thousands of guns and bullets, tanks and planes reached Israel safely. Although the world was watching Israel and her neighbors, the secret was kept.

Meanwhile, under Ben-Gurion's direction, Israel's own factories had been making more and more weapons.

But in July there was bad news. Prime Minister Nasser of Egypt seized the Suez Canal and said it belonged to Egypt. From then on the Egyptians would decide whose ships could use the canal; no longer would the canal be open to the ships of all countries. The Israelis knew their ships would not be allowed to go through the canal.

By October many people in both Israel and the Arab countries thought there was going to be a war again. Nasser announced that he was "fighting not only against Israel but against international Jewry...," a term used only by those people who hate the Jews.

After this, Ben-Gurion thought it was time to act.

CHAPTER TWENTY-FIVE

Thousands of people all over Israel disappeared on Thursday, October 25, 1956.

A secretary in a bank went out for lunch and did not return. An Ambassador complained that his chauffeur had left without telling him. Store managers apologized because their customers were not waited on quickly.

"We're sorry, but we've lost some of our salesmen," they said.

The day before, Egypt, Jordan and Syria had agreed to put their armies under the command of Prime Minister Nasser. This forced Ben-Gurion to make a very important decision. He had a choice: either let the three nations attack Israel or order Israel to attack them first. He decided that Israel must attack.

During the next few days he told some of his colleagues what he was going to do, but no one else.

On Thursday secret orders went out for people to come to their army posts. That was why so many of them had disappeared.

On Friday the officers of the southern command of the Army were told about the plan. They were going to be in charge, and they had just three days to get ready.

By Saturday most of the men who had been called to the Army were on their way to the Negev Desert. Chief of Staff Moshe Dayan, who had become one of Ben-Gurion's favorites, went over the final plans for the attack.

That same day the Prime Minister began to feel sick. He felt hot and he had a headache, but he stayed at his desk all day anyway. In the evening he called some of the members of the Cabinet to his home and told them his plan. They all thought the plan was a good one.

Ben-Gurion went to sleep that night satisfied that everything was going well. But he felt as if he were burning up with fever. On Sunday morning he was not well enough to leave his bed, but he got up because he felt it was his duty to see that his plan was carried out. Later in the day a full Cabinet meeting was held and the rest of the members heard the news for the first time. There was no disagreement about the plan. They all supported the Prime Minister.

Throughout the meeting Ben-Gurion took medicine, but it did not seem to be doing him any good. The red flush of his face showed that the fever had not gone away, and he had pains in his head and body.

After the meeting he told President Ben-Zvi what had been decided and then got into an automobile with Paula and Argov to drive over the twisting road to Tel Aviv.

When they arrived, Paula urged him to go to bed right away, but he insisted he could not. There were so many people coming to see him. First he received some members of the Knesset and explained to them about the plan, as he had already to the Cabinet and the President.

Then four doctors came in to examine him. They said he had a virus infection and ordered him to bed at once. Paula told him there was no need for a nurse; she would take care of her husband.

Ben-Gurion spent the afternoon propped up in bed giving final orders to the army officers and government members who paraded up the stairs, through the library, and into his bedroom.

All during Monday the street in front of the Ben-Gurion house was lined with parked cars. Once again the Prime Minister's bedroom and the library next to it began to fill up with officers and members of the Knesset and the Cabinet who wanted to see him.

In spite of the medicine the doctors had given him, the fever had not gone down.

About four o'clock in the afternoon he turned to General Dayan. He was thinking about the Israeli soldiers who were going to be carried to Sinai in airplanes and then parachute to the ground and surprise the Egyptians.

"What time do they jump?" he asked his chief of staff.

"At quarter after five," Dayan answered.

"Why so early?"

"Because if they jump after it's dark many will get hurt on the rocks," the chief of staff explained.

At a quarter after five they all glanced at their watches, then looked silently at each other. Everyone was wondering how the attack would turn out. The next fifty-five minutes—until messages began to arrive from the battlefield—seemed like hours.

At ten minutes after six a messenger brought the first report. It said:

"Our Dakotas have dropped the men on target and have returned unharmed."

The target was the Mitla Pass, in Sinai, only a short distance from the Suez Canal.

"I am worried about what will happen to this battalion," said Ben-Gurion, propped up in bed.

Fifteen minutes later a messenger brought in the second report.

"The drop has been successful," it said. "No enemy forces are to be seen within fifty kilometers. No Egyptian plane has tried to stop us."

Ben-Gurion gave a sigh of relief and picked up one of the books on the table beside his bed and began to read.

From then on there was a constant stream of messages, mostly from the battle front.

At nine o'clock in the evening he ordered the first announcement to the people of Israel and the rest of the world:

"Israeli forces have struck into the heart of Sinai and are more than halfway to Suez."

After this announcement a blackout of Israel was ordered. So Israelis spent most of Monday night covering their windows with dark curtains and then pasting strips of paper over the windows.

That night, Paula insisted Ben-Gurion be moved downstairs so he could be near their air-raid shelter. After all, the Egyptians might take their revenge by bombing Tel Aviv, so he would be safer downstairs.

Israel's officers had learned that the Egyptian Air Force now had about two hundred and thirty planes. If this force were sent against Tel Aviv, the city would be almost completely destroyed. Yet Ben-Gurion did not really want to move downstairs. He did because it would keep his wife from worrying about him.

On Tuesday he awoke early, feeling a little better. But the doctors said it would be best for him to remain in bed.

That morning he was handed a report that Egyptian planes had attacked the Israeli Army. This was

Ben-Gurion meets with President Kennedy in 1961. *(Consulate General of Israel)*

Among Ben-Gurion's great friends was France's champion of liberty and freedom, General Charles DeGaulle. Here they are seen visiting together in Paris. *(Israel State Archives)*

Ben-Gurion meets with West German Chancellor Konrad Adenauer in New York in 1960. The dramatic reconciliation of their two nations was opposed by some Israelis. *(Consulate General of Israel)*

Here is Ben-Gurion attempting to stand on his head and apply the lessons of Moshe Feldendrais. *(Jewish Observer and Middle East Review)*

Ben-Gurion led Israel's enthusiatic support for an international Bible contest. Seated with him from left to right are Teddy Kollck (later Mayor of Jerusalem), Yitzhak Navon later President of the State of Israel, and on the other side of him Itzhak Ben-Zvi, then the President of the State of Israel. *(Israel State Archives)*

Ben-Gurion owned the largest private library in the State of Israel. He loved his books and read every one of them. In retirement his favorite spot was his study.
(Israel State Archives)

Few photographs capture the expression of delight that often crossed the Prime Minister's face as does this one where once again Ben-Gurion is attending the birth of a newborn Israeli citizen. *(Israeli State Archives)*

Ben-Gurion was always enthusiastic around children. *(Israel State Archives)*

The Ben-Gurion family. *(Israel State Archives)*

Paula Ben-Gurion
hosting a tea.
(Israel State Archives)

A pensive Ben-Gurion
(Israel State Archives)

Though Ben-Gurion and Menachem Begin were political foes, he was prepared to sit down and break bread with him during the crisis that arose in 1967. Here at luncheon is Ben-Gurion, General of the Air Force Ezer Weizman, who later became President, and Menachem Begin, then leader of the opposition and later Prime Minister.
(Israel State Archives)

Ben-Gurion makes a point during an animated discussion. *(Israel State Archives)*

bad news. Now he would have to change his plans. He had given orders that the Air Force was not to fly across the Suez Canal, attack enemy soldiers, fire on enemy airplanes, or bomb enemy cities. This was because he thought that these things would lead to a big war. They might even set off a third world war. He had hoped that the war would not become bigger. But now that enemy planes were shooting at his soldiers, he ordered the Israeli Air Force to protect them.

On Wednesday he received news that an Egyptian warship, about eight miles at sea, had tried to fire on the port of Haifa. But all the shells had exploded in the water just a little short of land. The Egyptian ship was named the *Ibrahim el Awal*. She was now being chased by an Israeli ship.

The next report said a sea battle was taking place between the two ships. The Egyptian ship had been hit several times. Israeli planes were overhead. The *Ibrahim el Awal* was on fire.

Then the Egyptian crew surrendered and the Israelis towed the *Ibrahim el Awal* into Haifa.

But bigger news came later that day. Because Egypt had seized the Suez Canal, Britain and France suddenly turned Ben-Gurion's little war into a big one. They attacked Egyptian airfields and the Suez Canal itself.

The attack destroyed a large number of Egyptian planes, so the Israelis no longer had to fear that their cities might be bombed. Most of them, including the Prime Minister, went to bed that night quite happy.

On Thursday a stream of prisoners and captured Egyptian weapons began to arrive from the battle-fields.

On Friday the Prime Minister's secretary, Yitzhak Navon, received a telephone message:

"The entire Sinai Peninsula is in our hands."

He ran to Ben-Gurion's bedside to tell him. But the Prime Minister was deep in thought. There was a great storm of anger at the United Nations. Most of the countries were demanding that the British, the French, and the Israelis withdraw at once. Almost the whole world was condemning the Sinai attack.

On Monday, just one week after the paratroopers made their jump into Mitla Pass, a message came from the commander: their plan had now been carried out and it was a success. A thousand Egyptians had been killed, and less than two hundred Israelis. Only one Israeli had been taken prisoner by the Egyptians, but six thousand Egyptian prisoners had been taken by the Israelis.

On Tuesday, after nine days in bed, Ben-Gurion got up, dressed, and wrote the speech he was going to make to the Knesset the next day. On Tuesday, also, Great Britain and France decided to withdraw their troops, as the United Nations had demanded. That left only Israel.

On Wednesday, Ben-Gurion arose even earlier than

usual and drove to Jerusalem. He was still not completely well, but he stood on the platform, talking to
the Knesset for almost an hour, while Paula stayed
close by with a jar of strong coffee in case he needed
it to give him strength.

For most Israelis this was a time for rejoicing. But
their Prime Minister warned them that they should
not be overjoyed, for everything was not yet settled.
He told them they would have to be strong, because
the Arab rulers still wanted to get rid of them, and
also because they were not going to give in to the
U.N.'s demand.

On Thursday he felt very tired; still he started to
work at seven o'clock in the morning. There were so
many important things to be done.

An emergency Cabinet meeting was held at eleven
o'clock. It lasted two hours. Then Ben-Gurion went
home. He was happier now because he had decided
to stand firm, and his ministers in the Cabinet had
agreed that he was right.

He was having lunch when a note from President
Eisenhower arrived. It was more like a personal letter
than an official message from the leader of another
country, yet the President's words were very plain. If
Israel did not withdraw, she would be making it very
hard for the United Nations to bring peace to the
Arab nations and to Israel. The U.N. would blame
her for ignoring its rules after she had promised to
obey them. Israel might even be punished.

The letter changed everything. When Ben-Gurion
read it a second time, he knew that he would have to
give in. This would be one of the hardest things he
ever had to do.

It had been more than ten years since Ben-Gurion
had seen Dwight D. Eisenhower. He had been General Eisenhower then, and Ben-Gurion met him when
the general was making a tour of German camps
where Jews had been held as prisoners. He had liked
the honesty of the general then, and he felt now that
he could trust him.

But it was going to take a great deal of courage
for him to tell the Cabinet he had changed his mind,
that now he thought they should give up Sinai.

Then there was the Army. It had never been forced
to withdraw before. The officers and men would be
very disappointed, and even angry. They might not
understand why it was necessary to give up Sinai.

There were also the people. Winning Sinai had
made them very happy. Now when he asked them to
give it up, they might even think he had betrayed
them.

But, in spite of all these things, he had to do it.
Israel could not live without America's help and
friendship.

So that evening the Prime Minister sent a letter to
the President, saying that Israel's soldiers would leave
Sinai and allow United Nations troops to come in.
He also decided to tell this to his people over the

radio the same night. For several hours Ben-Gurion sat at his desk, writing his speech. When it was finished he read it aloud, and a recording was made of it just before midnight. It was to be broadcast in a half hour. Many announcements about it had been made on the radio. Everyone was urged to stay awake to hear it.

The Prime Minister's secretary, Navon, brought a small radio into Ben-Gurion's office. Several of the Cabinet members came in and sat down. Someone brought in coffee. Then all of them, together with Ben-Gurion, waited for twelve-thirty, when his speech would be broadcast to the whole country.

Just before air time, Ben-Gurion picked up one of the telephones on his desk and dialed a number. When a voice answered, he said:

"Paula, I promised to wake you up in time. The broadcast will begin in five minutes."

It lasted a half hour. As Ben-Gurion sat back listening to himself he seemed relaxed. One more important decision had been made.

CHAPTER TWENTY-SIX

One week during 1957 newspapers and magazines all over the world carried pictures of Israel's Prime Minister standing on his head on a beach near Tel Aviv. Some people thought it was a joke, that it was not really Ben-Gurion. The pictures were not very clear, so it might have been any short man with white hair. But it turned out that it was the Prime Minister, and this is the story of how those pictures came to be taken.

One day a professor from a school in Israel introduced a man named Moshe Feldenkrais to the Prime Minister. Feldenkrais was an expert on jujitsu. In fact he had written several books about it. Jujitsu is the art of training a man's muscles so he can do almost anything with them he wishes, and it began in Japan a long time ago.

Ben-Gurion was interested in jujitsu, but still he was a little skeptical of all the wonderful things

Feldenkrais said a man could learn to do by practicing jujitsu exercises.

"I want proof," he told his visitor.

Feldenkrais said he could give Ben-Gurion a list of people he had taught, or copies of his books. Or perhaps a few sample lessons?

"I'll read one of your books," Ben-Gurion decided.

A few days later he sent for Feldenkrais. He wanted to learn jujitsu.

"How many lessons will it take?" he asked.

"Ordinarily one lesson a week for a year is enough," Feldenkrais answered. "But I have never had a pupil over seventy before. You may be too old to change your ways."

But Ben-Gurion wanted to try, so they agreed that he would have a lesson for one hour each day when he came home from his office.

During the first lesson Feldenkrais showed the Prime Minister how to lie on his back on the floor with his eyes closed, raise one leg, and turn it slowly in half circles. At the same time he was to pay close attention to the movements he was making.

After the second lesson, Ben-Gurion was impressed and said to Feldenkrais:

"Maybe you have something."

This did not change Paula's opinion. She had been unhappy about the whole thing from the beginning and nicknamed Feldenkrais "Mr. Hokus-Pokus." She told him that she thought he was wasting a lot of her husband's valuable time with "all this monkey business of yours."

After a few more lessons, just when Ben-Gurion seemed to be doing very well with the exercises, he caught a cold. Then he went to Jerusalem, where the temperature was below freezing, and he got even sicker.

The next time Feldenkrais came to the house, Paula greeted him more sarcastically than usual.

"*Shalom*, Mr. Hokus-Pokus. You can't see him tonight," she said. "The doctor says he has pneumonia."

But Ben-Gurion heard them and called from his room:

"If that's Feldenkrais, I want to talk to him."

When Feldenkrais saw how sick the Prime Minister was, he gave Ben-Gurion some breathing exercises to do instead of the regular lesson. But Paula stood by to protect her husband.

"You mustn't make him work tonight. He's sick," she insisted.

"I am sure I can bring down his temperature," Feldenkrais answered.

Paula laughed.

"I used to be a nurse and I don't believe it," she said.

So they made a bet. Paula took Ben-Gurion's temperature, and then Feldenkrais began to give him the breathing exercises.

After ten minutes they took his temperature again. It had dropped one degree. But by this time Ben-Gurion was tired and a little annoyed.

"Go away and leave me alone" he said.

That ended the lesson for the night. But after a few weeks he was well enough to begin the lessons again.

He was very busy during this time, but he issued orders that nothing was to interfere with his daily appointments with Feldenkrais.

Paula was still unhappy about the lessons.

"I don't like people who are too much interested in themselves," she said to Feldenkrais. "You are making my husband too conscious of how he stands, how he walks, how he sits."

But, after a while, as she saw that the exercises were improving his health, she was no longer unhappy about them. She even sent other people to take lessons from "Mr. Hokus-Pokus."

For months the only person besides Paula, the professor, and the two secretaries who knew about the lessons was President Ben-Zvi, who happened to come in one day during an exercise.

The secret might never have leaked out if Feldenkrais hadn't taken a trip away from Israel. Just before he left he had been showing Ben-Gurion how to stand on his head. The Prime Minister could do it on a bed, but couldn't yet do it in the middle of the floor.

Several weeks later Feldenkrais was reading a newspaper in London and saw a picture of Ben-Gurion doing a perfect headstand. He telephoned to Tel Aviv. The Prime Minister said to him:

"I thought the beach would be soft like a bed, but extensive like the floor of a room. And it worked. I had no idea anyone ever saw me."

He felt wonderful. One day he went to a meeting with several young men from the government. When they entered the building where it was to be held, he asked the young man next to him:

"What floor are the offices on?"

"The fourth," the young man answered.

"The rest of you ride in the elevator," said Ben-Gurion. "I'll walk."

When they all reached the fourth floor, one of his companions told him the elevator man was disappointed because he had wanted the honor of taking the Prime Minister up.

"All right," said Ben-Gurion. "I'll ride down with him then."

CHAPTER TWENTY-SEVEN

It was a chilly, gray day in Jerusalem.
Because it was exactly a year before that the Sinai
campaign had started, the inspector general of police
ordered extra policemen to guard the Knesset. There
might be trouble.

The meeting that was going on inside was an
ordinary one. One member was making a speech,
and as he talked a few other members drifted out of
the room to get coffee and cigarettes.

There was a long table with chairs in the middle
of the Knesset, surrounded by tiers of seats for the
members and then a balcony for visitors and newspapermen. The chairs around the long table were for
the Prime Minister and the thirteen Ministers in his
Cabinet.

On this particular afternoon several of the Ministers were absent. But the Prime Minister was hunched
down in his chair, thinking. Argov, his military secretary, had gone to Tel Aviv for the day.

In the balcony there were a few students, some soldiers and tourists, and an unemployed waiter who was tired of walking around in the streets and had come in to watch the meeting.

The man who was speaking was I. Raphael, the tallest member of the Knesset. He was talking about the danger Israel had faced just the previous year.

Suddenly a young man with dark brown hair and a pointed nose jumped up from his seat in the back row of the balcony and threw something toward the Cabinet. It whizzed past the head of the Prime Minister, just missed the table, and fell near the chair of Moshe Shapiro, the Minister for Religious Affairs and Social Welfare.

Mr. Raphael stopped speaking in the middle of a word. For a moment there was complete silence. Then a voice in the balcony said:

"What nerve! Throwing a stone."

Minister Shapiro turned to look at the thing at his feet.

There was a loud explosion. Shapiro fell back in his chair. Blood was streaming from his head and stomach.

Foreign Minister Golda Meir gasped and clutched one of her legs with both hands.

Immediately the Prime Minister commanded in a loud voice:

"Sit down! Don't leave your seats." Blood was

turning one leg of his trousers dark red, and there was blood running down one of his arms.

A smell like gunpowder filled the room. In the balcony the guards grabbed the brown-haired young man as he was running toward a door.

There were two doctors in the Knesset , and they made their way down an aisle to the people who were hurt.

Several minutes later an ambulance came. Shapiro was carried out to it and taken to Hadassah Hospital. Mrs. Meir's foot was bandaged with handkerchiefs. Some pieces of steel had gone into Ben-Gurion's right arm and leg, but he insisted on walking to a car that took him to the hospital.

In the Knesset the police began to investigate. The thing that had been thrown was a grenade. If it had landed on the table it probably would have killed the Prime Minister and all the Cabinet Ministers who were there. It had made a deep hole in the floor and small holes all over the ceiling. One man in the balcony had been hurt.

The young man who had thrown the grenade was Moshe Ben Yaakov Dueg. He had come from Syria. The police found out that when he was a small child "he had had an accident that hurt his mind." After that he always acted strangely. Trying to kill the Prime Minister and the Cabinet had been his own idea, and no one had helped him.

As the story was told in the newspapers and on the radio, the people of Israel sighed with relief, for they had been afraid that perhaps Moshe had been working for the Arabs or for a group like the Stern Gang of years past. Instead they learned that he was only a poor crazy young man and so he was put away where he could do no more harm.

In the meantime, the Prime Minister was in Hadassah Hospital. Argov was very upset because he had been away when his chief was in danger, and he quickly returned from Tel Aviv when he heard the news. He and Paula watched over the Prime Minister. They let very few visitors see him: only his children, President Ben-Zvi, a young girl named Mazal who took care of the house in Jerusalem when the Ben-Gurions were in Tel Aviv, and the doctor.

On Ben-Gurion's second day in the hospital the Minister of Industry and Commerce came to call. As he came toward the door of the Prime Minister's room, Paula stood in the way.

"You can't go in," she told him. "I'm not admitting anyone but doctors."

As the Minister stammered that he was sorry, she added:

"It's easy to get past those policemen downstairs, but nobody's getting by me!"

That morning, Ben-Gurion told Argov to bring him all the mail from the office. The first letter he wrote was to the mother and father of Moshe Dueg.

It was not easy to do, for it was his right hand and arm that had been hurt. Yet, slowly and carefully, he wrote:

To the Parents of Moshe Dueg:
I know that you regret, as do all the people of Israel, the abominable and senseless crime which your son committed yesterday. You are not to blame. You are living in Israel, where justice reigns, and I hope that nothing untoward happens to you or your sons. Would that you succeed in educating the rest of your children to good deeds and to love Israel.
(signed) David Ben-Gurion

Nehemiah Argov was constantly at the Prime Minister's bedside during the first four days after the explosion in the Knesset. By Saturday, Ben-Gurion was in good spirits, and the doctors said he would be able to leave the hospital very soon. Argov had some work to do at the Defense Ministry, so he drove to Tel Aviv. Later that day, as he was driving back to Jerusalem, a wasp flew in the car window and stung him on the eyelid. For a moment he looked away from the road, and just then his car hit a man on a bicycle.

Argov stopped the car and ran out onto the road. The man was unconscious. He picked him up and put him in the back seat. Then he drove as fast as he could to a hospital. The doctors examined the man and then told Nehemiah that he was hurt very badly. He had only a slight chance of getting well.

Argov found out that the man had been in Israel only a little while, and that he had come from Morocco to live in this new nation with his wife and four children. After that, Nehemiah drove back to Tel Aviv.

By Sunday he had not returned to Jerusalem. That day, officers of the Defense Ministry went to his apartment and knocked on his door. When they received no answer they broke the door down. They found Nehemiah sitting at his desk, dead. He had shot himself in the head with his army pistol.

He left two notes. One was to Ben-Gurion. The other was to "My dear friends," and in it he wrote:

"Today I knocked down a cyclist .... I fear he will not live .... I cannot forgive myself for the suffering I have caused this family .... I beg his forgiveness and that of his family."

Then he asked that all the money he had in the bank be given to the man, or his widow if he didn't live.

When the news of Nehemiah's death was received in Jerusalem, Ben-Gurion's doctors talked it over with his staff. He had a fever after his operation, and the doctors did not want him to hear anything that might shock him and make the fever go up. So they decided to keep the bad news from him. The radio stations were told not to mention Argov's death on their news broadcasts because Ben-Gurion always listened to them. Then all the newspapers were called. Each one was asked to print one copy that didn't mention Argov's death. So great was the press' respect for Ben-Gurion that they did as requested. A messenger would pick up these papers right after they were printed and bring them to the hospital.

That evening a reporter called the hospital to ask about the bicyclist. He was told the man was now out of danger; he would live.

On Monday, Argov was buried with full military honors. Six colonels carried his coffin to the grave. There were several hundred people at the funeral. One of them was Paula. But Ben-Gurion was reading quietly in his bed at the hospital, unaware of what was going on.

Finally, on Tuesday, the doctors decided he could be told. Chief of Staff Dayan was chosen to do it. He went to Ben-Gurion's room with the doctors and several of the Prime Minister's friends.

Ben-Gurion was in a cheerful mood, for he was to leave the hospital soon. He talked eagerly with his secretary, Navon, but finally Dayan said:

"We have bad news for you. Nehemiah is dead."

Ben-Gurion turned pale. He sat upright in bed and demanded in a shocked voice:

"What did you say?"

Dayan told him what had happened and then gave him the sealed letter Nehemiah had left.

Ben-Gurion opened it slowly. As he read it, his eyes clouded. Finally, as he came to the last page, he turned in bed until his back was to the others in the room. The visitors looked at one another embarrassed. They had never seen him like this before. One by one they quietly left the room.

At last he was alone with his sadness. The wounds in his arm and leg suddenly began to hurt again. But the hurt in his heart was greater, for he knew there was no man to take Nehemiah's place.

Many days later Ben-Gurion showed the letter to a few friends. It didn't mention the accident. It was filled mostly with words of the love and admiration Nehemiah had for his commander. He thanked Ben-Gurion for his friendship and said he never felt he deserved the honor.

"I know my action will cause you pain, but I cannot do otherwise," he wrote.

He admitted it was not the deed of a strong man. Ben-Gurion was a strong man, and needed strong men around him. He, Nehemiah, was no longer a strong man. He begged his commander to go on leading the people. They needed him, and he alone could guide them.

For days after he heard about Nehemiah, Ben-Gurion lay still in his bed. He did not eat or sleep, and he refused to talk to the people who came to see him. The doctors thought it might be better if someone could persuade him to talk about Nehemiah.

Maybe then he would lose some of his sadness. Paula and the children asked Yigael Yadin to try.

Renana was there when he came into Ben-Gurion's room. Her father had his face to the wall. Suddenly he turned and saw Yadin. He forgot his sadness for a moment and asked:

"Have you finished your diggings at Hazor?"

"Yes."

"Tell me about them," Ben-Gurion said.

Yadin talked a long time about this ancient place he had been digging up. It had been the largest city in the Holy Land in the days of Joshua. Then he stopped. This was not the reason he had come. He looked straight into Ben-Gurion's sad eyes and said:

"Let's talk about Nehemiah."

The Prime Minister shook his head, but Yadin insisted. Then, little by little, Ben-Gurion began to talk about Nehemiah. But that did not make his sadness disappear. For weeks he seemed like a different man.

In the hospital there was much competition among the nurses as to who would take care of the Prime Minister. A dark-haired young woman named Edna was his day nurse when Navon, his secretary, came in one day. He watched her for a little while and then said:

"You must get over the idea that you are taking care of a Prime Minister. You must not let him order you around. You order him. Treat him like an ordinary sick man."

Ben-Gurion was listening.

"But I am not a sick man," he said.

"All right," Navon said to nurse Edna. "Then you treat him like an ordinary well man."

When Ben-Gurion left the hospital, two weeks later, one foot was still in bandages, and this was the way he limped into the Knesset to make his first speech since he had been hurt. He began by saying:

"I am very sorry that for two days a grievous misfortune, the loss of Nehemiah, was concealed from me. I am sorry, but not angry....

"For about ten years Nehemiah and I worked together....

"Nehemiah, like myself, was not perfect. There are no perfect men in the world. Even the Bible does not describe any perfect man.... Every man has good and bad qualities...

"What was unique about Nehemiah.... was that he had one quality to perfection.... devotion and loyalty.... Nehemiah was endowed with a rare and precious gift, the gift of great love....

"Permit me to stand here, alone, silent, for a brief moment, in respect to his memory."

CHAPTER TWENTY-EIGHT

In 1958, Israel reached her tenth anniversary with Ben-Gurion still guiding her firmly. A twelve-month round of festivities began: parades, balls, music and dancing, sports contests, and carnivals.

There was mass jumping from airplanes by the parachute troops who had landed in Sinai, airplanes flying in formation, and displays by ships in the harbors.

In April the visitors began to arrive for the celebration. They came from every part of the world. There were so many of them that on some nights there was hardly a bed in all Israel that was not being slept in. With the visitors came reporters, photographers, people who wanted to make films for the movies and television, and magazine writers who wanted to see the Prime Minister. He answered thousands of questions, posed for hundreds of pictures. Several times the reporters asked him if he would be willing to meet with President Nasser. He answered:

"I will go to Cairo to see him any time he invites me. I would not hesitate to negotiate with him, man to man."

Ben-Gurion told those who came to see him the story of Israel's first ten years. Almost a million immigrants had come in. Israel had almost two million people now. What country, anywhere in the world, had doubled its size in only ten years?

They had come from seventy countries, speaking almost every language known to man, even Japanese. But they learned Hebrew quickly. Hundreds of villages had been built, and many thousands of houses.

Israel now grew most of the food her people ate. There were steel mills at the ancient city of Acre.

Even in science and the arts Israel had much to be proud of. She had six orchestras, many theaters, painters, poets, singers, and a school for atomic scientists.

But Ben-Gurion talked about the future, too. In another ten years he wanted a million more immigrants to come to Israel. Many more people should go to the desert and help make it green with fields and trees. Israel should build a strong navy. The way ahead might still be hard, but as long as he lived, as long as he was the leader of Israel, he would always be urging his people to do more to make their country beautiful and strong.

The part of the celebration of Israel's tenth birthday that Ben-Gurion thought was the most important of all was a contest to find out who had the best knowledge of the Bible. First, contests were held in many countries. The winner in each country would come to Israel for the finals, and there the world champion would be picked from among the national winners.

One hot Monday in August the contest to pick Israel's winner was held in the largest auditorium in Tel Aviv. Every one of the thousands of seats was taken. The contest was also broadcast, and the Prime Minister sat for four hours in front of his radio, listening to the questions that were asked and the answers the contestants gave. Half a million other Israelis were listening also.

The winner was a young man named Amos Hacham. Amos had been born in Jerusalem. When he was a boy he had had an accident, and because of it he dragged one leg when he walked, and his mouth had been hurt, so it was hard for him to talk. But Amos knew the answers to almost all the questions and won the contest easily.

The next day, as usual, Amos went to work at his job in the Jerusalem School for the Blind. But something very extraordinary happened. He received a telephone call, and the voice said:

"The Prime Minister would like to see you as soon as possible."

He borrowed a suit and a white shirt from a friend and hurried to the Prime Minister's office. There Ben-Gurion greeted him warmly.

"I must tell you, Amos, that hearing the quiz over the radio was for me, as a Jew, a wonderful experience, and I am sure the entire nation shares this feeling," the Prime Minister said. "You, Amos, have enhanced the glory of Israel, and we are all proud of you."

He told Amos that he must not be discouraged about how hard it was for him to talk.

"I have been learning about speech control myself. There is something you can do about this," he said. Then he arranged for Feldenkrais to give Amos lessons.

After that they talked a long time about their favorite subject, the Bible.

Several weeks later the fourteen other winners arrived in Israel for the final contest. There was a Baptist from Georgia, a school teacher from Brazil, an Italian girl who came with the Pope's blessing, a Protestant from Mexico; and there were others, from Finland, France, Argentina, South Africa, Colombia, Luxembourg, Holland, Sweden, and Uruguay.

The questions began one morning and were still going on at midnight. The last four hours were broadcast. Almost every radio in Israel was tuned in. The prize for the winner was a greenish vase two thousand years old that had been found in an ancient tomb. The excitement everywhere in Israel was great that night. Ben-Gurion himself was as excited as anyone.

The questions were hard, but Amos Hacham won, in spite of his trouble in speaking. The French school-teacher was second and the Brazilian third.

The next day, Ben-Gurion was very proud.

Soon after that he had another reason to be proud. Each year Hadassah, the Women's Zionist Organization of the United States gives an award to a famous man or woman. Once Eleanor Roosevelt had received the award, and another time, Justice William O. Douglas of the United States Supreme Court. In 1958 the award was presented to David Ben-Gurion. Here was the leader who had helped create Israel and make her a strong nation. He had given his people new hope for the future. In recognition of all this, the Hadassah award said:

"Man of action and man of thought, his life has been dedicated to the survival of the Jews as a people, and the establishment of Israel as a state, and to the rights of man everywhere...."

CHAPTER TWENTY-NINE

On a hot summer day in 1959, in the Knesset in Jerusalem, Ben-Gurion made one of the most important speeches of his life.

Israel had started to build its own munitions factories. She did not want to be always dependent on outsiders for her defense.

The biggest order so far had come from West Germany. It was for $3,300,000 worth of grenade launchers.

When the news leaked out, some Knesset members accused the government of "selling arms to the devil."

There was a danger that the country would be torn apart. Some cool, clear voice was needed to calm the storm.

Ben-Gurion spoke for a long time to the members of the parliament.

"The Germany of today is not the Germany of Hitler," he told them.

He finished by saying:

"It is our duty to take any steps possible to safeguard our peace and security."

As he sat down there were both cheers and jeers. Then they voted.

Ben-Gurion was opposed by 45 members, but 57 supported him. He had won a great political victory.

But members of two leftist parties in the Knesset had voted against him. This was in violation of an agreement they had signed.

Ben-Gurion was so angry that he resigned as Prime Minister.

This meant there must be an election. It would be the first general election in four years.

The campaign was a long, hard one. Ben-Gurion was almost 73 years old. But he campaigned as vigorously as a young man.

His party was running against nineteen other parties. Each party had its long list of candidates.

Ben-Gurion asked three young men to help him.

One was Moshe Dayan, who lost an eye fighting with the British in World War II and who recently served as Chief of Staff of the Army. People knew him wherever he went because he had to wear a black eye patch the rest of his life.

The second was Shimon Peres. He had been director of the Defense Ministry under B.G.

The third was Abba Eban. Ben-Gurion had named him Israel's Ambassador to the United Nations in

New York, and then Ambassador to Washington. Now Ben-Gurion asked him to give up being a diplomat and become a politician.

They formed a very good team. Soon the country was calling them "the Old Man and his boys. "

When the campaign ended B.G. went to his kibbutz at Sde Boker. He was tired and wanted to rest.

On election night he did not even wait up to listen to the returns.

The next morning when he turned on his radio he got the happy news. He and his party had won the greatest victory of his long career.

They had gained strength. They would now have 47 instead of 40 seats in the Knesset.

CHAPTER THIRTY

In 1960 Israel and its Prime Minister were more popular in the world than ever before.

The Soviet Union was still backing the Arabs. But all the other important countries were solidly behind the Jewish State. Ben-Gurion found this out when he went on a tour of the western capitals.

The day before he arrived in Washington, ten Arab Ambassadors paraded into the White House. They said:

"Ben-Gurion is coming to poison American minds." They said it was a plot against the Arabs. President Eisenhower listened to the Arabs and nodded politely.

The next day when Ben-Gurion called at the White House he made no demands. He did not ask for anything. But he did tell the President that Russia was giving Egypt a great many MIG-19s, its latest jet fighters.

Eisenhower said Ben-Gurion should not worry. If

anyone attacked Israel, the United States would come to her help. Immediately!

"But we don't want American soldiers to die for us," Ben-Gurion said.

Eisenhower replied that he was a former general. He said Israel alone could not possibly hold off her enemies.

Ben-Gurion replied: "We can take care of ourselves if the United States will just supply us with guns."

The President had a busy schedule that day, so Ben-Gurion was told he could stay only 30 minutes.

It was two hours before the Prime Minister and the President finally said "goodbye" to each other.

In New York Ben-Gurion called on Chancellor Konrad Adenauer of Germany at the hotel where he was staying. It was a strange meeting. One man represented the country that a few years ago had killed six million of the other man's people.

Before their meeting the two men had exchanged many letters and Ben-Gurion had decided that Adenauer was "one of the greatest statesmen of our time."

This was because he had helped Germany recover politically and morally after the Nazi disgrace.

Adenauer on his side felt a great friendship for Ben-Gurion.

In Paris Ben-Gurion met with General Charles de Gaulle. The French president told the Israeli Prime

Minister that France would rush to Israel's help in any emergency.

Again B.G. said:

"Give us munitions, not men."

When they posed for press pictures de Gaulle's face was almost a foot away from Ben-Gurion's face because of the great difference in their height. In that meeting the two men sealed a personal friendship that would last the rest of their lives.

Later de Gaulle told his friends he thought Ben-Gurion and Adenauer were the two great leaders of the West.

CHAPTER THIRTY-ONE

One day Ben-Gurion was talking with a 15 year-old Israeli boy named Yigael.

"What do you know about the Holocaust?" the Prime Minister asked his young visitor.

"I know what they say about it, but I don't believe it," Yigael replied.

"You don't believe that the Nazis killed six million Jews?"

"No I don't," the boy said. "It's just a story they made up to make other people feel sorry for us."

That night Ben-Gurion said to his wife Paula:

"I'm afraid a whole generation has grown up since the war that doesn't know, or has forgotten, or just doesn't believe."

The year was 1960.

Israel's intellegence had been looking everywhere for Adolph Eichmann. He was the Nazi army officer who had charge of shipping millions of Jews to the death camps. In those camps they had been gassed and their bodies burned in large ovens. They finally found Eichmann hiding in Argentina, in South America.

Ben-Gurion knew it was no use asking Argentina to turn Eichmann over to Israel. He knew they would simply refuse. So Ben-Gurion decided to order his secret agents to kidnap Eichmann and bring him back to Israel to stand trial. It was one of the most serious decisions of Ben-Gurion's life. He knew many people would say that kidnapping is against the law. His answer was: "Eichmann was one of the chief villains in the greatest crime against the Jews in all history. It is only right that he should be put on trial in the Jewish state."

The kidnapping was a great success. It was kept a secret until the Nazi officer had been flown all the way from South America to Israel.

"We must give him a very fair trial," Ben-Gurion said. "We must show the world what Jewish justice is."

Hundreds of reporters came from America, Europe, Asia and even from Africa to attend the trial. It was held in a building in Jerusalem that looked like a theater. On the stage there was a bullet-proof glass booth for Eichmann which was to protect him from being shot by some fanatic.

The Nazi Eichmann sat for four months inside that booth listening to hundreds of men and women tell about his crimes. Finally Eichmann was found guilty. The three judges ruled that he should be hanged for his part in killing the six million Jews.

After the execution, Ben-Gurion said:

"For the first time in Jewish history justice has been done by the sovereign Jewish people."

The trial was Ben-Gurion's way of telling Yigael what really happened during the Holocaust.

CHAPTER THIRTY-TWO

Ben-Gurion had many serious political problems in 1961. But he pushed them all aside for awhile and took his wife, Paula, on a 31-day tour of western countries. Wherever they went in the United States B.G. was treated as if he were the head of some great nation.

President John F. Kennedy had just moved into the White House. He had many very serious problems of his own. Yet he talked for 90 minutes with the Israeli Prime Minister.

In New York the Ben-Gurions had a suite of rooms on the 35th floor of the Waldorf Towers. Hour after hour, day after day, a parade of famous people came to see them.

Former President Harry Truman came. He had helped Israel get started by recognizing the new state right after it was born.

The Mayor of New York City came and the Governor of New York State.

Many Senators and labor leaders came, also the leaders of Jewish organizations.

Then the Ben-Gurions flew to Canada in a Royal Canadian Air Force plane.

In Ottawa they were greeted by Canada's Prime Minister. Also by the diplomats of 30 countries. Even the Soviet Ambassador came.

Ben-Gurion told the Canadians how he had visited their country 44 years ago, during World War I. He was a Jewish soldier in the British Army. He went through Canada on his way from the United States to the Middle East.

After he addressed the Canadian Parliament he had a private talk with Prime Minister John Diefenbaker. It was supposed to last one hour. At the end of an hour and a half the Canadian Prime Minister asked the Israeli Prime Minister to talk with him for two or three hours the next day.

When they got to London, England, it was the same story. More cheering crowds. More long talks. More honors by the government. Then a long meeting with the British Prime Minister Harold Macmillian.

In Paris General de Gaulle gave a luncheon for the Ben-Gurions in the famous Elysee Palace. The French President raised his wine glass and said:

"It is always good for men of good will to see each other and reach agreement, "

Then he drank a toast to "Israel, our friend and ally."

The trip lasted just over a month. Ben-Gurion said it was a chance for Paula "to see the world." It also helped make Ben-Gurion and Israel more popular than ever, no matter where they went.

CHAPTER THIRTY-THREE

Soon after Israel was founded, Ben-Gurion had a visit from U Nu, Premier of Burma.

Ben-Gurion, a Jew, and U Nu, a Buddhist, were both proud of their heritage and they got along very well together.

They talked about how both Israel and Burma became independent states about the same time. Burma was the 58th state admitted to the United Nations. Israel was the 59th.

Ben-Gurion said to U Nu:

"I have always considered Buddha one of the greatest figures in history." They talked for hours about religion and philosophy. That meeting was in 1955.

Six years later Ben-Gurion returned the visit. For six days he was Premier U Nu's guest in the Burmese capital of Rangoon.

There were state luncheons, formal dinners, garden parties and receptions. Most of the time Ben-

Gurion wore a sarong, the Burmese native costume. U Nu took his Jewish guest to see the spectacular pagoda called the Shwe Dagon. Ben-Gurion was so impressed with its beauty that he gave a thousand *kyats* (about $200) to a fund to re-gild the golden dome.

After the six days in Rangoon Ben-Gurion agreed to participate in a retreat. For the next eight days he obeyed all the very strict rules laid down by his host. For eight days he lived in a small room with not much furniture. No books to read. In this room a simple meal was served to him every noon.

Every few hours U Nu himself or a Buddhist scholar would pay him a short visit. The rest of the time Ben-Gurion was supposed to sit in silence. He was told to think about the mysteries of life.

Once when Ben-Gurion and U Nu were having dinner alone, the Burma Premier told how Buddhists love not only humans but all living creatures.

Ben-Gurion pointed to the food on the table and said with a smile:

"But you are eating fish and meat."

Now U Nu smiled and said:

"Those are Chinese dishes made to look like fish and meat. They are not really fish and meat. They are 100 percent vegetables."

Ben-Gurion's main interest in Burma was discussing with U Nu the differences between Judaism and Buddhism. The two men agreed that Jews and Buddhists both have an equal desire for peace. Also an equal feeling about the brotherhood of man. And an equal respect for truth.

When the visit was over the two leaders issued a joint statement. It said they were both against the world's arms race. Also, against the big differences in how poor people and rich people live. In the statement they promised to work for peace and for a better life for the poor.

Ben-Gurion did not have a great sense of humor, but in his own book of memoirs, when he wrote about the statement he and U Nu had issued he said:

"U Nu is a good Buddhist and the Israeli Prime Minister is more or less a good Jew, so I am sure that both men mean every word of that statement."

CHAPTER THIRTY-FOUR

Germany gave Israel munitions factories many orders in the 1960s for Israeli sub-machine guns. It was called an Uzi. This is the first name of the man who invented them.

In 1963 the West German Defense Minister, Franz Josef Strauss, was invited to pay Israel a visit. The right wing Herut party and the Israeli Communist party made noisy demonstrations in the streets of Tel Aviv and Jerusalem. They demanded a cancellation of the visit. Ben-Gurion stood firm. He persuaded the Knesset *not* to cancel.

The German Minister came one day late, on purpose. He hoped to avoid any crowds of protesters. Communist lawyers demanded that Minister Strauss be arrested. They said he was a war criminal.

Ben-Gurion answered them. "Near the end of the war he (Strauss) was a commander at a German anti-aircraft school. That was hardly a war crime."

Strauss said: "I have a clear conscience." He promised to work for an exchange of ambassadors with Israel. While he was on a 10-day tour of the country, wherever he went Israeli Communists and Herut party members marched in the streets with banners.

Ben-Gurion said to these demonstrators: "The Jewish people will not accept Hitler's racial theory. A man should not be accused of something just because he belongs to a certain people."

One day in 1963 members of the Ben-Gurion cabinet met at the Prime Minister's office for an ordinary weekly meeting.

Ben-Gurion rapped for order.

When the talking stopped he said:

"I am resigning."

Someone asked:

"As Prime Minister?"

Ben-Gurion replied:

"As Prime Minister and also as Minister of Defense."

It was his eighth resignation in the 15 years he had been guiding the country.

Many people thought this was just another resignation to frighten his political enemies. But then he said:

"I am also giving up my seat in the Knesset."

Then they knew he was serious. Ben-Gurion was now 77. Many younger men had retired. However,

B.G.'s good friend Adenauer was 87 and he was still in office.

Maybe Ben-Gurion was unhappy. He had failed in his ambition to cut down the number of political parties. He had not succeeded in changing the voting system so it would be like America's. Maybe he was unhappy because so few young people had come from Europe and the United States to live in the desert. Or maybe he wanted to spend the rest of his life reading and writing and studying.

So the Old Man and Paula packed up and went off to live on the kibbutz at Sde Boker.

That same year Ben-Gurion's first real book was published. It had a good title: *Israel, Years of Challenge*. Today there are hundreds of cards in the file of the Library of Congress in Washington under "Ben-Gurion." All these books are either *by* or *about* Ben-Gurion.

CHAPTER THIRTY-FIVE

Ben-Gurion no longer had a political job, but he was still a politician.

In 1965 he had a political fight with his own party, Mapai, and he quit the party. Then he formed his own party called Rafi. Those letters in Hebrew stand for "Israel Workers' List." Ben-Gurion was now almost 79. This was rather old to be the leader of a new young party.

One newspaper said: "He is like an old volcano. He refuses to become extinct." He was joined in Rafi by Moshe Dayan, the man with the black eye patch. Also by Shimon Peres, who would become Prime Minister years later. Also by Teddy Kollek, who later became Mayor of Jerusalem. Also by many other young men.

In the next election they hoped to get the most seats in the Knesset.

They campaigned from Dan to Beersheba. They gave hundreds of speeches.

But when the election was held they got only 10 seats. The other 110 seats went to their rivals.

In 1966 Ben-Gurion had his 80th birthday and one of his friends said: "He's not an old man of 80. He's two young men of 40."

Even newspapers that had opposed him began calling him "The Grand Old Man."

One paper told a story of how Ben Gurion and Ho Chi Minh of Vietnam were friends in Paris in the 1940s. They lived in the same hotel. Both men were revolutionaries in those days. Both wanted independence for their people. Each day Ben-Gurion would climb two flights of stairs to visit Ho Chi Minh. Or Ho Chi Minh would come down two flights and call on B.G. They talked about the dreams they had for the future.

On his 80th birthday many other stories about B.G. popped up.

He once wrote love poems and signed them "The Dreamer." For a short time in his youth he was a drama critic. In the days when the Turks occupied Palestine he studied Turkish. He hoped to become a member of the Turkish Parliament and help the Jews get their land back from the Turks.

CHAPTER THIRTY-SIX

In the spring of 1967 everyone knew there would soon be another war.

Egypt's President Nasser had an ambition to be the head of the entire Arab world. His photograph hung in the windows of houses and shops in half a dozen Arab countries.

Many times, in Egyptian newspapers and on Egyptian radio, he promised the Arabs he would lead them in a war to wipe Israel off the map.

After the war in 1956, a U.N. peace-keeping force was stationed in the Sinai desert between the Egyptians and the Israelis. This was a guarantee of peace.

But in May of 1967 Nasser broke the signed treaty and demanded that the U.N. soldiers be removed. This was a signal that he was about to make war.

Several weeks later Nasser's troops closed the Gulf of Aqaba. The Egyptian President then announced that no Israeli ship would be permitted to sail through the Gulf.

This created an unbearable situation for Israel. Her only lifeline to Africa and Asia had been cut.

What Nasser did was an open act of war.

Next he sent eighty thousand of his Arab soldiers and nearly one thousand tanks across the Sinai desert, right up to Israel's frontier.

Now, for the first time since 1956, Israeli and Egyptian soldiers stood face to face.

Arab troops started marching from Iraq, Algeria and Kuwait in Israel's direction. Saudi Arabia sent some of her soldiers to the Jordan-Israeli frontier.

Syria began shelling the *kibbutzim* around Lake Kinneret.

It was the greatest military crisis in Israel's history.

Big headlines in the newspapers said:

BRING BACK BEN-GURION

For 20 years Menachem Begin, leader of the Herut party, and Ben-Gurion had had a political feud. They never even said "Shalom!" to each other.

But now Begin said he would forget the past if Ben-Gurion would come back as Prime Minister.

Ben-Gurion agreed to return on certain conditions, but some of the other politicians refused his offer.

And so the Old Man, who had been the military and political leader in Israel's first two wars, was on the sidelines in this one.

The first day of the war, in just 80 minutes, 374 Egyptian planes were destroyed.

The war was all over in six days. Israel had won a tremendous victory.

All of Jerusalem was now part of the Jewish state. Also, all of Judea and Samaria, which had importance for religious Jews.

Ben-Gurion joined the rest of the country celebrating the victory.

But there were more than one million Arabs in the occupied territories. And no Jews. This worried the Old Man.

"We have no need for all this extra land," he said. "We were not meant to rule over other people."

Sde Boker, November 1959.
(© *David Rubinger*)

Ben-Gurion State Funeral, December, 1973
(© *David Rubinger*)

At his funeral, the principal eulogy at the gravesite was delivered by Prime Minister Yitzhak Rabin. Seen in the front row of mourners is Golda Meir and next to her is Shimon Peres. *(Israel State Archives)*

The gravesite of Paula and David Ben-Gurion.
(Israel State Archives)

Getting ready for an Academic Convocation at Ben-Gurion University.
(Tslila Zagagi)

The beautiful landscaping at Ben-Gurion University has won Israeli Architectural awards
(Tslila Zagagi)

Arial views of the Ben-Gurion University campus in Beer-Sheva.
(© *Albatross*)

Israeli Prime Minister Yitzhak Rabin, received a honorary degree from Ben-Gurion-University in 1994. He is seen here with Ben-Gurion University President Avishay Braverman.

Ben-Gurion University President Braverman awards Honorary Doctoral degree to South African President, Nelson Mandela in 1997.
(© *Albatross*)

Ben-Gurion University of the Negev.
(© *Albatross*)

CHAPTER THIRTY-SEVEN

One chilly day in 1968 Ben-Gurion's wife Paula was taken by ambulance from the kibbutz to a hospital in Beersheba. She died the next morning. For about 50 years Paula had never been far away from her husband's side. He depended on her for protection that no armed guard could give him. She treated him the way a good Jewish mother treats her favorite son.

Now she was gone and Ben-Gurion was very sad. The fire was gone from his eyes. The spark that made him such an extraordinary man was no longer there. The bounce was gone from his step.

He resigned his seat in the Knesset. Now he spent all his time living in the past and writing his memoirs. After one year the old Ben-Gurion began to come back slowly. He was now almost 83.

Once more he tried to interest young people to come down to the desert. He told them how exciting it is to be a pioneer. He *knew*, because he had been a pioneer himself when he came to Palestine as a very young man.

On October 16, 1970, Ben-Gurion celebrated his 84th birthday. Crowds of people in Tel Aviv and Jerusalem took the day off to trek down to Sde Boker. It was the best birthday party Ben-Gurion had ever had. Even his political enemies said it was time for them to make peace with the former Prime Minister. On that day in 1970 Ben-Gurion became The Grand Old Man of Israel. He was now the link between the pioneers who settled Palestine 60 years ago and the Israel of today.

Ben-Gurion often told people he saw no sense in a necktie. He liked to wear an open-neck shirt and no jacket.

But on his 84th birthday he greeted the crowds wearing a dark suit, a vest and a tie. He even *looked* like an Elder Statesman.

CHAPTER THIRTY-EIGHT

One of Ben-Gurion's last interviews was with an American writer, the author of this book.

We sat together in the study of his house at Sde Boker. The walls were lined with books to the ceiling. This was his favorite room.

The Old Man refused to move to a fancy apartment in the College of the Negev that he had helped create.

He was at home in this simple, old house. He liked it. Here he had received heads of state, ambassadors, television crews and the Secretary General of the United Nations.

At the start of the interview he told me that the book I was writing about him should be more about the future than the past.

As he talked about his vision of Israel, he seemed more like a prophet than ever. His eyes sparkled and he looked young again.

"We Jews are different from other people," he said. "We are a unique breed."

"Because we are the people of the Bible, we have certain special qualities."

"The rule of law is more important to us than to other people. That's because Judaism is based on the laws of Moses."

"We are a diverse people. We are not all alike. For that reason we must always practice tolerance, one for the other."

"Those who are religious should have tolerance for those who do not happen to be religious."

"And those who are not religious should have more tolerance for those who live by the religious laws, as they see them."

"We must always be concerned with values."

"We must always be more interested in quality than quantity. "

Then he told me about how Moshe Dayan came to him several years after Independence and suggested that Israel should extend her frontiers by attacking Jordan.

"I told him 'no!' I told him we should not want to rule over more territory. I told him that what we need is not more land but more Jews."

Much of our conversation was about the Negev. Whenever Ben-Gurion talked about the desert he leaned back in his chair and seemed to be looking far off into the future.

"In the Negev we must build a big industrial center," he said.

"Someday millions of men and women and children will live in this part of Israel."

"Of course most people don't like to live in a desert. We must make the desert attractive for young pioneers."

"We must build many schools."

"We will change sea water into fresh water."

"We will have lots of agriculture in the Negev. We will irrigate with sea water after we take out the salt."

"We will have cheap power."

Ben-Gurion told me he thought China would soon be one of the greatest countries in the world.

"In small Israel we have all the problems of the big nations. Little by little we are solving them."

"We must work hard to improve our country in every way."

Ben-Gurion's secretary-bodyguard said some other people were waiting to see the former Prime Minister.

The Old Man waved the bodyguard away. He still wanted to talk about the future.

He had promised me 30 minutes. Already he had talked for 60 minutes.

His last words were:

"We must work hard to be the chosen people—to be a light unto the nations."

CHAPTER THIRTY-NINE

In 1972 tens of thousands of Russian Jews began coming to Israel.

This was a dream Ben-Gurion had had for years.

Israel was created to be the homeland for *all* Jews, but many Jews who had good educations and good jobs in other countries did not want to leave to go to Israel. The Jews of Russia, however, were eager to leave, and many of them were doctors, scientists, professors—people that Israel needed badly. But the Russian government had not allowed them to leave for Israel.

Now the gates were open a little and he was happy.

But there was still no peace in the Middle East.

Egypt's President Nasser died of a heart attack. His successor was Anwar Sadat. But the new President at that time was just as warlike as the old one.

Israel's borders were being violated almost every day by Arab gunmen. They shot up schools, buses, *kibbutzim.*

Ben-Gurion hoped that the Arabs would respond to Israel's peace moves. But instead of accepting Israel's suggestion that they meet at a negotiating table, they chose the battlefield again.

The war of 1973 began on Yom Kippur. Everyone in Israel was taken by surprise. Ben-Gurion was just as shocked as everyone else.

When the Syrians and Egyptians attacked, the Old Man spent a lot of time studying military maps.

Now he no longer had Paula to make sure that he ate properly. Or that he got enough sleep.

He was 87 now. Younger men were directing the army. Younger men were making all the decisions. They no longer consulted Ben-Gurion before they acted. This bothered him.

Now his life was books and his writing.

Of course he followed the battle news every hour. But in between he worked on his memoirs.

The war began as a disaster.

But it ended with the Syrians and the Egyptians pushed back almost to Damascus and Cairo.

Now Israel could relax. The danger was over.

Now Ben-Gurion could give all his time—not just part of his time—to his memoirs.

CHAPTER FORTY

On Sunday, November 18, 1973, Ben-Gurion was taken to a hospital in Tel Aviv. His entire right side was paralyzed. The doctors said a blood vessel in his brain had broken. They called it a "massive cerebral hemorrhage."

The next day the doctors said: "Condition serious, but he's not in danger." The Israeli doctors predicted that if Ben-Gurion lived he would always be paralyzed.

The Old Man had hardly ever admitted defeat. This time the odds were very much against him. The paralysis made it impossible for him to speak. He had lost the use of his right hand, so he could no longer write.

When a visitor came into his hospital room he would smile a greeting. Then he would hold out his left hand. After almost a week of helplessness he became only partly conscious. It was only a question of time.

His son, Amos, and his two daughters sat beside his bed. Or in the hallway just outside his room. They were there on Saturday, December 1, when the doctor said: "He has stopped breathing."

The Builder of Israel was dead.

As soon as the news was flashed around the world, cables began to pour into Jerusalem and Tel Aviv. Presidents, Prime Ministers, Governors, Senators and Jewish leaders by the hundreds sent messages of sympathy. Flags were ordered flown at half-mast.

The body was taken to the Knesset building in Jerusalem. There it lay in state as 200,000 Israelis paid their final respects to The Grand Old Man.

Then the coffin was flown to Sde Boker. There the body of David Ben-Gurion was placed in the earth beside the grave of his wife Paula.

It was called "a private service." But 300 political and military leaders and the representatives of some foreign governments and a few friends of the family were present.

Ben-Gurion himself had said he wanted a very simple funeral. The army chaplain gave a short prayer. For one minute sirens all over the country wailed the message that the great David Ben-Gurion had been laid to rest.

The next day in New York 19,000 people jammed into Madison Square Garden for a Ben-Gurion tribute. The Mayor told them: "Ben-Gurion was the Maccabee of modern times."

One rabbi said: "He walked like a giant. He left his imprint on the pages of history."

A few days later the name of Israel's international airport was changed. Instead of Lydda or Lod it would now be called "Ben-Gurion Airport." The name of the University of the Negev was changed to "Ben-Gurion University of the Negev."

If he were still alive David Ben-Gurion would have been 100 years old on October 16, 1986.

He had been dead for almost 13 years by the time of the centennial birthday party. But the world remembered.

George Washington is called "the father of his country'

David Ben-Gurion deserves to be called "the builder of Israel."

He, more than any other one person, helped make a 2,000-year-old dream come true—the dream of a Jewish state in the land of David, Solomon and the Prophets, a state built upon the eternal Jewish vision of justice, peace and equality.

Largely because of his work Jews throughout the world sing "Am Yisroel Chai!" "The People of Israel Live!"

BEN-GURION IN HIS OWN WORDS

*F*or many people, David Ben-Gurion was a modern day prophet and teacher.

He had a clear vision that Israel must become a model nation—a beacon of hope to the world.

His fervor, his ideals, his wisdom, confirm what history now knows: Israel's first Prime Minister was truly the "Builder of Israel."

These excerpts show how Ben-Gurion remarkably anticipated some present controversies and how he prescribed a sensible course of action for Israel.

After reading "In His Own Words," you will learn a little more of what he valued, what he emphasized as Israel's leader, and you will have some ideas of how Israel today will have to deal with current issues and challenges.

On relations with Israel's Arab neighbors

History has pronounced us neighbors; and it is not merely a geographical closeness. There is much

nearness in language, culture and history. Coopera-
tion between the Jewish people in its Land and independent Arabia is an historical necessity, and it will
come about, for the Arab people need it no less than
does Israel. It is feasible only on a basis of equality,
mutual respect and reciprocal aid. It will convert the
Middle East into one of the cultural centers of the
world, as in Bible times it was. Each of the two
peoples has something to offer the other, without
giving up anything of its own. This productive exchange will be a boon to both, to the Middle East
and the whole world.

On the dignity of man

Man, according to Jewish belief, was created in
the image of God. There can be no more profound,
lofty or penetrating express of the greatness, the worth
and the dignity of man than this. The Judaic concep-
tion of God embodies the ultimate of goodness,
beauty, justice and truth. To the Jewish people the
life of a man was sacred and dear. Men who were
created in the image of God are equal. They are an
end in themselves, not a means. The image imposes
a duty. It is no wonder then that this nation's think-
ers based the Torah on one great rule —"Love your
neighbor as yourself." Love of one's neighbor did
not mean only of the fellow Jew: "But the stranger

that dwells with you shall be as one born among you, and you shall love him as yourself: For you were strangers in the land of Egypt."

On respecting and tolerating the religious practices of all Jews

Differences of opinion in the spiritual field, which is precisely where differences penetrate to the very depths, must be treated with the utmost seriousness. All sides are certain that they are faithful to the sources and roots of Judaism, as they understand them, and there is no supreme and unbiased Jewish court to decide between them, nor would any of them, for that matter, accept the verdict of such a court if it actually did exist. They must live together and build up the nation and the State together, without inflicting their own opinions upon others.

On the challenge of Negev enterprise

More than half the expanse of the State in the south is entirely barren yet, and in that barren area perhaps lie buried the richest natural treasures to be found in the Land. One such treasure has been discovered, and we had begun to exploit it in part - the treasure of the Dead Sea. But there are many others hidden and blanketed by the sands, and we must unearth and work them. The Negev enterprise, possibly the greatest and most difficult of all, demands a driving power and a bold initiative, a majestic pioneer resolve, the likes of which no other enterprise ever required....

The great energy, the courage and the constructive initiative of Jewish youth, and the scientific and technological capacity of Israel's scientists and research workers, will have to overcome these natural difficulties, and develop the South and the Negev for large-scale settlement, based on pasture, agriculture, handicrafts, mining and industry, fishing and shipping - exploiting all the resources of the scientific discoveries and technological progress of our day.

On the role of pioneering ("halutziut")

And the most wonderful and most powerful instrument through which man gains the mastery over nature is man himself. The potential in this wonderful being has no parallel among all the complicated and extraordinary instruments and machines that man has created. And it is only as the result of an intuitive understanding of man's potential, and the capacity and the will to make use of these possibilities— which we call *halutziut* or pioneering—that we have succeeded in our enterprise in this country...

On the role of Israel toward its immigrants, "partners in destiny"

The spiritual absorption of this immigration, the molding of this human clay into a cultured, creative, independent nation, aspiring to a vision, is not an easy task. Its difficulties are not less than those of economic absorption. It needs a gigantic moral and educational effort, and a profound and pure love, to unify these neglected people, to share with them our national treasures and values, to integrate these once remote and oppressed communities into our society, culture, language, and creativeness. This we must do not as dispensers of charity, but as partners in destiny.

On Hebrew education

Hebrew education involves not only teaching the language, but also imparting the greatest of the Jewish classics of all generations, and first and foremost the Book of Books, which is the summit and pride of Jewish creativity. It is the first and foremost foundation of the faith and moral teachings of Israel, from which all the creative work of the generations that followed drew its sustenance and in which they saw the proud heritage of the Jewish people.

On the bond between Jews living outside Israel with those living in Israel

The intensification of the personal bonds between Jews living outside Israel and Jews living in Israel is needed: visits; capital investments; sending children, youth and student to study in Israel for a longer or shorter period; and, above all, the training of the best of our youth and our scientists to join the builders and defenders of Israel and to play a personal part in the creative and redeeming work that is being carried out in this country.

On Jewish spirit

Faith and belief in the supremacy of the spirit have accompanied the Jewish people throughout its long journey down the years, from the revelation on Sinai to our own War of Liberation. This faith was held by all the great men of Israel, who shaped the Jewish nation from its very beginning, who created and fostered its Torah, its song, its prophetic aspiration, its literature, its justice and its laws, its ultimate vision and the messianic hope which strove for its unity and its national and universal mission. It was held by the men who led Israel's wars of spiritual and political independence and who, sanctifying the Name, perished in the massacres of Jewish communities during the Crusades, at the stakes of the Inquisition, in the pogroms of Chmelnitzki and in Nazi holocausts. It was held by the men who founded, built and developed the work of settlement, which led to the State of Israel.

On competing by relying on the strength of spirit

We can compete in the supremacy of the spirit, in standards of culture, science and technique, so that they be not the exclusive property of a few individual specialists, experts and professionals, but the common heritage of every worker in field and forge, office and school, airport and seaport, on land and at sea. Without this kind of supremacy of the spirit we shall not make the desert bloom or maintain our security; we shall not keep our place in the world nor be faithful to our historic trust. In the long view, however, it is spiritual power that decides; in the kingdom of the spirit it is not quantity that counts, but quality.

On the Jewish vision of national and universal redemption

At a very early date the Jewish people conceived an idea, an original epoch-making thought, of which there was nothing like it among the peoples in the East or the West, among neither the people of Egypt, Babylon, India or China nor of Greece or Rome or their descendants in Europe to our times. Our people did not long for the past as other primitive people did, for the legendary Golden Age gone without return; they turned their gaze to the future, to that final day when "the earth shall be full of the knowledge of the Lord, as the waters cover the sea" and the nations shall beat their swords into plowshares and "nation shall not life up a sword against nation, neither shall they learn war any more"....

Not a feeble longing for an imaginary splendor of the past, but a vision of the future, a vision of a reign of justice and peace among all nations— this was the historical philosophy which the Prophets of Israel instilled in their people. This expectation and belief in the future sustained our people in the hour of distress and affliction throughout their long history and brought them to this point, to the beginning of their national redemption, in which there is the first glimmering of redemption for the whole of mankind.

On using the heritage of the past, the achievements of our time, and the promise of the future

Without the heritage of the past, the great heritage of the Prophets of Israel, our lives would be separated from the source of their vitality, and a vacuum would be created around us and within us; but this heritage is absorbed and merged in the new and ever-renewed achievements of the spirit of men. The stream of life and historical change can never come to a stop. During the centuries in which we have played our part on the world's stage we have learned from many nations, and although we are bound by unbreakable bonds to the ancient past of our people and its great heritage in the prophetic age and thereafter, yet we are sons of our own time. Just as we are a link in the chain of the generations of Israel, so we are members of the family of nations and a part of the human race in our own time. In our lives, in our undertakings and culture, in the society we wish to build in our renewed homeland, we must make use of everything good, useful, true and beautiful that we can find either in the heritage of the past or in the achievements of the human spirit in our time and the days to come.

On having vision

We have it in us to build in the Homeland a Jewish people which men everywhere will praise - its life, economy, society, culture, and internal and external policies based on the teachings of the Prophets, the lessons of justice, mercy and peace. This is the moral imperative of our past, the imperative of our attachment to all Jews, the political imperative of our place in the world. In this vision is the secret of our survival, our resurgence. Where there is not vision, the people perish.

BEN-GURION'S LEGACY

O f all the monuments and places in Israel that honor David Ben-Gurion's lifetime of accomplishments and leadership by carrying his name, none would have pleased him more than Ben-Gurion University of the Negev (BGU). The University, which is located in Beer-Sheva, is one of the most dynamic universities in the world, an internationally recognized institution of scholarship and research.

Many readers of this book will someday be taking a trip to Israel and may even consider studying there in the future. Let's take a brief tour of a unique university that captures the spirit of David Ben-Gurion's quest for excellence and his love of the Negev region—Ben-Gurion University.

Beer-Sheva is a thriving metropolitan area of 180,000 people in 1998, and the capital of Israel's Negev Region, which comprises more than 60 percent of Israel's land. The Patriarch Abraham settled

in Beer-Sheva, which was an ancient central cross-
roads, and it was here that he planted a tamarisk tree
by a well after he made a pact with Abimelech. That
ancient well site can be visited today.

Beer-Sheva is Israel's fourth most populous urban center, and future plans call for as many as one
half-million people to live within the Beer Sheva metropolitan area within 20 years.

This area of Israel contains one of the most unusual ethnic mixes in the world. Here immigrants
from North Africa, Ethiopia, India, Europe, North
and South America and the republics of the former
Soviet Union along with Bedouin Arabs and Jews
born in Israel coexist.

Upon entering the main campus, one is immediately taken by the stunning architecture of campus
buildings and the beautifully landscaped areas. It is
like a flower in full bloom. One can feel the vitality
and mission of this University by talking to faculty
and students, who are not only involved with tradi-
tional university objectives of teaching and research,
but who are fully engaged in services that are clearly
relevant to the social needs of the development of
Beer- Sheva and the Negev region. Thus, David Ben-
Gurion's impassioned plea to make the desert bloom
has become a reality through this University named
in his honor.

BGU student enrollment has expanded dramatically in recent years and now there are over 13,500 full time students engaged in studies that lead to Bachelor's, Master's and Doctorate degrees. The student body reflects the mixture of ethnic and social backgrounds of the Negev and also draws students from the center and north of Israel. BGU is the leading Israeli university working to absorb new immigrants and narrow the social and cultural gaps among diverse communities within the country.

A eclectic, engaged group of scholars and scientists make up the various faculties and schools of the university, which include the faculties of Humanities and Social Sciences, Natural Science, Engineering Sciences, Health Science, School of Management, the Chaim Herzog Center for Middle East Studies and Diplomacy.

The relatively low student-to-faculty ratios allow for a personal approach to learning. Research or course work in the humanities and social science may take students to such diverse places as *kibbutzim*, immigrant absorption centers or urban renewal projects. Students in the sciences work on problems of immediate importance to Israeli society that may include environmental problems and strategies for plant, animal and human adaptation to arid zones and application of new sources of energy.

Ben-Gurion University is home to the Joyce and Irving Goldman Medical School, an extraordinary institution which seeks to attain a balance between medical education, science and health care. This world renown approach, known as the Beer-Sheva experience, trains physicians to be sensitive to personal and community needs and at the same time offers state of the art medical training.

In 1998, Ben-Gurion University of the Negev will jointly offer with Columbia University Health Sciences a four-year medical degree program to teach doctors special skills in primary care, cross-cultural, community, and preventive medicine. It will be the only M.D. program that emphasizes preventive and community medicine as they relate to international health.

The Sde Boker campus is located 30 miles south of Beer-Sheva, adjacent to Kibbutz Sde Boker, where Ben-Gurion lived from 1953 until his death in 1973. Paula and David Ben Gurion's final resting-place is located at Sde Boker, and today that honored place is within a national park with a breathtaking desert vista.

The Sde Boker campus is also home to two major research centers. One is the Jacob Blaustein Institute for Desert Research. It has become the world leader in combating desertification, which is the disastrous trend of land areas to become arid wastelands. Scientists from all over the globe come here to pursue specialized desert research. The Blaustein Institute has become a way for Israel to build bridges to new friends in arid lands worldwide. In this sense, David Ben-Gurion's call to Israel's scientists to unlock the secrets of the Negev to help others has become a reality. The many programs of the Institute represent the University's commitment to contributing to world well-being and nurturing ties of friendship between Israel and other peoples of the world.

In 1976, the Israeli Knesset passed the David Ben-Gurion Law establishing the Ben-Gurion Heritage Institute. Located at Sde Boker, the Institute is committed to the development of creative educational programs promoting the values of the founders of modern Israel and is also entrusted with the preservation of Ben-Gurion's home at Sde Boker. The Institute's varied programs have had a profound impact both in Israel and among Jewish communities throughout the world, insuring that future generations will understand and appreciate Ben-Gurion's vision and legacy.

The Ben-Gurion Research Center, jointly established in 1982 by the University and the Heritage Institute, focuses on multi-disiplinary, academic research on the life of David Ben-Gurion and the establishment of the State of Israel. This Research Center is the other independent academic unit of the University, which shares a place at he Sde Boker Campus.

Ben-Gurion University's community action outreach program is enormously popular with students. Year after year, University students commit their time and efforts to focus on disadvantaged residents of Beer-Sheva like new immigrants, Bedouins, and children at risk. This commitment to a better society is a tribute to the University's loyalty to the Ben-Gurion ideal of a just society.

All qualified undergraduate and graduate students who are enrolled in an accredited college or university are eligible for the Ben-Gurion University overseas student programs. Graduating high school seniors who have been accepted to an accredited college or university are also eligible to apply. The program is available for a semester or full year program. Courses are offered in English. Students take Hebrew in a six week intensive *Ulpan* prior to each semester, and may continue their Hebrew studies during the course of the academic semester. Students who are fluent in Hebrew may also take regular university courses. There are opportunities for individualized research and internships in this overseas program. For additional information, you may contact:

Center for International Student Programs
Office of Student Services/NA
342 Madison Avenue, Suite 1224
New York, NY 10173
Phone 212-687-7721
E-mail: BGUOSP@haven.ios.com
Internet: http://www.bgu.ac.il/osp

The story of Ben-Gurion University of the Negev, naturally begins with Ben-Gurion himself, but the continuation of his legacy, is now in the hands of a new generation of leaders.

Ben-Gurion University has been blessed with great leadership—the administration, the faculty, the student body, and a host of world wide Associates organizations— which have lavished their energies, resources, and devotion in an inspiring partnership with Israel's youngest university. All of them, in their own way, have kept the promise and the dreams of David Ben-Gurion alive.